Women at Sea

by

Brianna Snider

Published by Brianna Snider at Women at Sea Publishing

Copyright Brianna Snider 2018

All rights reserved. No part of this book may be reproduced or transmitted in any form or by any means, electronic or mechanical, including photocopying, recording, or by any information storage and retrieval system, without written permission from the author, except for the inclusion of brief quotations in a review.

ISBN: 978-1539643739 Softcover

Create Space Edition, License Notes
Smash Words Edition, License Notes
This book is licensed for your personal enjoyment only. Please do not copy or reproduce. Thank you for respecting the hard work of this author.

Other editions available
This book is available in other formats at
www.womenatsea.ca

Dedication

This book is dedicated to my wonderful husband Blaine and two children Sienna and Kohan who support me in every way possible.

Disclaimer Please note the views and actions of the contributors are solely those of the contributors and not those of the author Brianna Snider. Some names of people and ships have been changed for privacy reasons.

Brianna Snider

Table of Contents

PROLOGUE...7
THE SEAGULL AND THE BOAT..............................10
BIG RED...16
FOR THE LOVE OF THE OCEAN..........................21
HONEYMOON IN ALASKA....................................25
THE SAILOR IN ME...30
ON TOP OF THE GREAT WALL OF CHINA....34
FIRE IN THE HOLE!..37
DON'T MISS THE BOAT!..43
IN THE ENGINE ROOM..47
TO PEE OR NOT TO PEE..50
BIOLUMINESCENCE...57
ABANDON SHIP..61
HAVING A RHIOT...66
THINK PINK..70
A SHITTY SITUATION..74
BETWEEN A BOAT AND A HARD PLACE........77
THAR, SHE BLOWS!..80
THE GREAT WHITE NORTH..................................85
ANCHORS AWAY IN MOZAMBIQUE.................90
PREGNANT AT SEA..96
DESCENDANTS FROM THE BOUNTY.............103
OLD TRADITIONS DIE HARD.............................107
SAILING WOES..110
THE LOCKS OF THE WELLAND CANAL.......113
LIFE IN MATZATLAN...116
THE WALLS HAVE EARS......................................119
SAILBOAT RACING...122

STUCK IN THE BILGE	*129*
T.V VALOUR	*134*
THE MAGIC OF SAILING	*138*
MAN, I FEEL LIKE A SAILOR!	*142*
A SAILOR'S CHANCE	*144*
THE HEART WANTS WHAT IT WANTS	*149*
FISHTAILING IN THE PANAMA CANAL	*154*
SAYING GOODBYE TO THE SEA	*159*
EPILOGUE	*166*
SO, YOU WANT TO BE A SAILOR NOW WHAT?	*169*
PACKING FOR SEA	*177-185*
RULES OF THE ROAD	*186*
HIERARCHY ON A SHIP	*189*
KNOTS, BENDS AND HITCHES	*193*
RULES AND SUPERSTITIONS	*202*
ASTRONOMY 101	*207*
THE WEATHER AND THE ENVIRONMENT	*210*
PHOENETIC ALPHABET	*215*
NAUTICAL TERMINOLOGY	*217*
MEET THE CONTRIBUTORS	*225*
ABOUT THE AUTHOR	*229*
REFERENECES	*232*

Women at Sea

Prologue

I am a woman. I am vulnerable. I cry, and I bleed. I have hopes, and dreams, and I believe I can make a difference in this world. What I have come to realize over the past few years is that a woman's vulnerability is the other side of her strength. As Eleanor Roosevelt once said, "A woman is like a tea bag. You can't tell how strong she is until you put her in hot water." (Roosevelt,1996)

Ever since I was a little girl, my mother, has always told me, "Never rely on a man for anything except love. Always make sure you can support and fend for yourself." And that was what I intended on doing. Supporting myself. I could do that, right? I was 21, newly single and looking for a challenge. Something rewarding. A job that would help people and help me make a difference. Of course, it wouldn't hurt if it paid well too.

Since I didn't have much of a college education, I decided to look to the trades as an alternative. I needed to find something that sparked my interest and ignited a fire inside me.

Brianna Snider

I have always been on, in, or around the ocean. My parents were avid sailors who sailed up to Alaska on a 27' Catalina sail boat for their honeymoon. I owe my love of the ocean to them. I was then born on that same sailboat. Ever since I can remember we have always had a boat. I also lived on a 50' powerboat for five years in high school with my family, including my 90-pound dog. What a different life! I was always drawn to the mysteries of the ocean and the magic and wonders it contains.

Not many people can say they have experienced what I have, but I guess I like that. My life, my experiences are what makes me stand out in a crowd. In this book, I list some of the challenges I've had to face being a woman at sea, and being a sailor. These pages contain the collective thoughts, emotions, and lessons, from several women occupying different positions on a vast array of vessels. By putting this book together, I hope to guide you as a reader, sailor or non-sailor, through the journeys of women working at sea in a world still very much dominated by men, and to invite you to feel what these individual women felt. The experience of being a sailor itself has its challenges: being away from home, being away from your loved ones, working long consecutive shifts. Throw the emotional waves that go along with being a woman on top of the physical and psychological mental stresses, and you will begin to appreciate what these women sailors have overcome.

The experience of meeting these women has been a life-changing one, and I have cherished the stories they chose to share.

I have tried to make this book light, funny and awe-inspiring, giving the reader a true and accurate perspective of each woman, I have interviewed, in addition to sharing my own experiences. Each chapter represents a new story.

Follow me along my personal sailing journey with multiple short stories throughout this book and meet 25 other amazing women along the way.

There is nothing quite like seeing a million stars up in the sky at night with no other ambient light, just quiet and undisturbed peacefulness. As you read on, you will discover the unique brand of sailor humour I have included just for fun. May you see many sunsets and sunrises out over the horizon and may you always be in a following sea.

The Seagull and the Boat

Sacrifices come with any job. Some sacrifices can include giving something up, trying to find a work life balance, physical injury, and most importantly your mental wellbeing. Some jobs can be stressful at times, and as first responders, can often lead to post traumatic stress.

As a young female who was vibrant, full of life, and who had a go-getter mentality, I am not surprised I ended up choosing a career that some people couldn't even imagine doing. My beanstalk figure, size 11 shoes, and marked complexion, made it somewhat difficult to fit in during my awkward high school years. Despite my challenges to fit in, I became very athletic in high school playing soccer, volleyball, basketball, track and field, and even became a high school wrestling champion. As you can imagine, sitting for eight-hours a day, five days a week, didn't appeal to me when I was deciding on my lifelong career. Before I made my career choice, I wanted to volunteer for something either after work or on the weekend to help me decide on my likes and dislikes and to be able to give back to the community. I had recently grabbed an application form to be a candy striper at the local hospital. I thought it would be fun and I had once thought of becoming a nurse. I then had one of my close friends at the time tell me that he just started volunteering for the Auxiliary Coast Guard and that he got to drive a RHIB (Ridged Hull

Inflatable Boat). I thought to myself, "Me drive a RHIB? Do fish swim?"

I jumped at the opportunity to drive a fast boat, help people in trouble, and (of course) get more experience on the water. Just because I had been around boats my entire life did not mean I knew how to drive one.

With the Auxiliary Coast Guard, I received the proper training, which included courses such as my Radio Operators Certificate and my Marine Basic First Aid Certificate. I didn't have to pay for anything, which was great. I was working during the day working a 9:00am-5:00pm job, so I was assigned the night crew. Our crew consisted of a total of four crew members, three crew and one coxswain. We were all given floater suits, reflective vests equipped with a knife, a strobe light, and a high impact helmet because we would be going so fast on the water.

I had to finish all the required training before I could even step foot on the boat. Once I was finished came the fun part. We learned how to drive the boat. Because I was on the night crew, we trained at night and we were on call from 6:00pm to 7:00am every day, every other week. We were told to bring a dry bag with extra clothes, food, and water for those especially long nights when we were out on a call.

Training was my favorite time of the week by far. I also learned how to tie knots, did man-overboard drills, practiced search pattern sequences, and learned how to par buckle, which is how to recover someone in the water with hypothermia; you must bring them up over the side of the boat side-ways.

We received a lot of boat handling experience to get used to the boat and be comfortable on the water to prepare for an incident. We would sometimes only get a Search and Rescue call out once a month, or sometimes as frequently as once or twice a week. One memorable Easter long weekend, we ended up getting called out three times in three days. That was unheard of in our unit. Our crew ended up getting a column and picture in our local newspaper because of it. We were famous! Nothing like a day in the life of a first responder.

Sometimes the calls would last only minutes, and then the Joint Rescue Coordination Centre who dispatched us would stand us down. Other times we would be on a call that lasted for hours.

In the summer of 2004, someone reported a boat drifting in the middle of the straight between Sidney Island and James Island with no lights, which was a hazard to marine navigation. If someone were to run into them because they couldn't see them it could be disastrous.

The Auxiliary Coast Guard was tasked by JRCC to investigate. We ended up coming alongside to the vessel with our RHIB to see if anyone was onboard. As it turned out, there was a man with his two kids sleeping onboard, no one was steering the boat. We ended up towing them back to a nearby marina but were only able to go a few knots/per hr. while towing, so it took us hours to get them back to land. That was nine-hours in the freezing cold, in the middle of the night, trying to comfort two small children, that I will never forget.

Some calls were flare sightings, others were people who had broken down and needed us to tow them to safety.

Sometimes after a long night on a call, I would have to call in sick the next day at work because I was either too tired or too sore. On one call we had, I was driving the RHIB for a couple of hours in rough weather conditions. I guess I didn't brace myself sufficiently because the next morning I literally couldn't move. I must have thrown my back out because I couldn't even get out of bed. I ended up calling in sick for the following three days after that because I couldn't even move. Unfortunately, the vibrations from the RHIB were hard on the body and a price I had to pay as a first responder.

Women at Sea

My work at the time was good about being on call every few weeks, they were considerate, and we had an understanding that I could leave work early if I were to get called out. Even though volunteering for the Auxiliary Coast Guard was hard on the body and often stressful, it was worth it in the end. It was so rewarding, and they made training fun and interesting. I have a lot of good memories of volunteering with them.

Summer of 2005, we had just got called out on a SAR call very early on a weekend day morning. I was driving the boat and as we made our way out of the harbor and started gaining speed, I suddenly blacked out and couldn't see anything. I was wearing my floater suit (head to toe) and running from my car down to the boat, having drank no water and eaten no food so early in the morning and was ready to pass out from over exertion. It didn't really hit me until I took the wheel and started driving the boat. A couple of minutes in, I couldn't see anything. It was all black. No matter how big I made my eyes, I just couldn't see anything. Finally, I grabbed my Coxswain by the arm who was right beside me at the time on the radio and said I can't see and pushed him towards the steering wheel. Just in the nick of time it seemed as I came tumbling down and fainted onto the deck.

My crew members gave me water and a snack to get me back on my toes and I was good as new. The lesson I learned that day was to always take care of yourself first. How can you rescue and care for others if you don't look after yourself first?

After my blackout episode, every time I stepped foot on the boat I made sure I had eaten and drank enough water. I was not going to play the victim again. I took my responsibilities of being a First Responder very seriously and didn't want to do anything to jeopardize what I loved to do.

At about 1:00am the pager went off one tepid summer night. We had just been called out on a call, one that I will never forget. I was sitting on the back seat of a RHIB going at a speed of about 40 knots/hr. in the pitch black with the odd star peeking through the sky. Seagulls like to sleep on the surface of the water in groups and we must have drove through a flock of seagulls sitting on the water. As soon as we neared them, they started to scatter and flew in every direction trying to escape being hit, nearly hitting us in the process. One seagull, was not so lucky to escape unscathed. It must have been disoriented in the night with the bright lights shinning from the boat. It flew right at us hitting the windshield of our boat, smack dab in the middle, and with us going at a speed of 40 knots/hr. we killed it instantly on impact.

With the wind blowing and the boat still going in a forward motion, the dead bird then whipped around the rest of the boat, landing in the back of the boat where I was sitting, and somehow ending up wrapped around my pant leg.

I started screaming, "Get it off, get it off!" and frantically shaking my leg to try and remove the dead bird from my leg that was covered in blood.

My coxswain Mark made his way to the back of the boat, grabbed the seagull off my pant leg, and chucked it overboard. There was seagull blood all over the deck and all over my pant leg and I kept screaming to get it off. With the wing span, the bird must have been close to four feet wide. It was much bigger up close than I ever could have imagined. That was one of the worst experiences I've ever had to endure out on the water and to this day, still haunts me.

Despite my woes and lousy experiences, I still loved being on the water. I loved the feeling of being free, and the feeling of escape from the mundane. It was final; I had to change something in my life. I decided I wanted to become a true sailor, not just a volunteer. I wanted to do this for my career. I was going to quit my day job, and go to school to become a sailor. I was going to follow my dream, my passion.

Women at Sea

Seagull perched on a log escaping the stormy day at Esquimalt Lagoon beach in Victoria, B.C.

-Photo courtesy of B. Snider

Big Red

Story by Sandra Vandenham

It pays to be nice. Whether they are a cook, steward, or the captain of the ship, you should treat everyone the way you want to be treated.

A well-fed crew-member is a happy crew-member. George, a burly man but as soft as a teddy bear and one of our helicopter pilots, was always happy and was always very friendly towards me. He always came down to the galley after hours for extra snacks. He joked around and was always bugging me to go flying in the helicopter with him.

"What a cool experience that would be?" I thought.

He must have asked me every day of that four-month patrol. At the time, I had asked my superiors, but they wouldn't give me permission. On a ship, you must obey your superiors and so that patrol, I went without.

I was the ship's cook on board a Navy warship, everyone called me Big Red. It might be because of my fiery red hair or the fact that I am built strong like an ox and could easily take anyone down, or maybe a bit of both. I didn't originally sign up to be a ship's cook. I had my nursing degree for geriatrics before I joined the armed forces. Wanting to explore what this world had to offer and see the different ports my ex-husband had always talked about during his career in the Navy, I decided to sign myself up for the armed forces and see what it was all about.

Women at Sea

My thoughts were that I would be doing something in the line of my previous profession since I had a medical background, but little did I know I was about to become a cook on board the ship. I survived the ten weeks of basic training that every recruit must endure, and came out of it feeling like a champ. They sent me to do 16 weeks of Cook training, which is really a two-year program crammed into 16 weeks. It was very intense, but we learned how to prepare gourmet meals for an entire ship's crew. We learned how to bake bread and treats, and I learned to always make sure there was food readily available for the crew including snacks at any time of the day. A well-fed crew wants to fight harder and come back home to their ship.

There I was, running down the flats of the ship chasing after a plastic bin full of frozen roasts that were supposed to be dinner for the entire crew in two days' time. All I could think was "we must have hit a rough patch of weather". Either that or someone was just learning how to drive the ship for the first time. That jolt or sharp turn, bumped the dinner I made and sent it gliding across the floor and had me chasing after it. Several crew members stopped to help me pick up the escaped meat. I learned from then on to secure everything down; after all, I was on a rolling ship.

Being a cook wasn't easy. A lot of the male crew members thought I shouldn't be there and asked why I left my nursing position to come and do this type of work. All the higher ranked crew looked down upon me for being a cook and gave me a rough time. I did have a few friends on board the ship, but they were mostly males. I didn't dare go near the other women on board in fear of their cattiness or monthly PMS.

During my time on the ship, I cooked for a lot of people. More importantly, I cooked for several dignitaries who came onboard our ship while we were docked in different ports all over the world. When we were docked in Esquimalt Harbor, I cooked dinner for Prince Edward of Great Britain. That was one of my most memorable experiences. How many people can say they have ever cooked for a prince? I also know that when we were in foreign ports, several foreign dignitaries came on board for dinner. I had to step up my game and make sure everything was perfect from taste to the presentation of the meal. I had to make sure the dinner was hot enough, that I didn't overcook the veggies, and that the meat was properly cooked to taste. It made me feel important and special, that my work had meaning. Working as a cook, I didn't feel important very often. Everyone has a right to be a part of the crew and have his or her duties matter. The crew would be lost if they didn't have anyone to cook meals for them. They wouldn't be able to perform their own duties without a proper healthy meal and probably would starve to death as most of them can't cook for themselves.

One night in the middle of the night I was awakened by a big poke. As I shared the mess where I slept with many other crew members, we all had to be quiet to not disturb one another. The lady who shook me asked if I had put my name on the list to go flying in the helicopter.

"Yes!" I exclaimed nearly falling out of my bunk.

"We have a spot ready for you if you're interested to come flying," she said.

"Do sailors drink?" I thought to myself.

Of course, my answer was yes. This was going to be the most exciting thing I've ever done as a cook on board the ship. I ran up to the hanger and the officers there asked me for my dog tags, and my visa card.

"I didn't know I had to bring them" I answered. "Can I run back and go get it?"

"Yes, if you hurry," they said.

I have never run so fast up and down stairs in my entire life. I quickly grabbed my dog tags and visa card and ran back up to the helicopter hanger on the ship. I was finally going to get my chance to go for a helicopter ride. I was so excited I could barely breathe.

Women at Sea

I was told before I left not to speak a word.

"Just sit and be quiet," the officers told me.

I quickly shook my head and agreed with them. When I finally got in, the pilot did his checks. He called out everyone's positions over the radio, and as he called your position you were supposed to say "Here" or something along those lines. When the pilot called "Cook" I didn't say anything. Remember, I was told not to say a word when I got in. I just sat there quietly.

"He's talking to you cook," the co-pilot said.

"Oh, I didn't know. I was told not to say anything when I got here," I said.

We all had a laugh and off we went up into the sky. So high and fast, it felt like we were floating up above the clouds and I could even see the ship down below that now seemed so small. I had never experienced anything quite like that in my entire life. While in the air, the pilot participated in a helicopter exercise of a vessel that went down and we had to search for people that fell overboard. Suddenly, the sliding door of the helicopter whipped open and the crew were hanging out the door to search and get a better look. By the end of the flight, the flight crew had made me an honorary crewmember because of my involvement with the exercise.

What a chance of a lifetime. I had so much fun and had so much to talk about when I got back. It was incredible. All because I was nice to the pilot and always had leftovers out for him to eat at night. What they say is true: "What goes around comes around." I learned that day that even the smallest gesture is appreciated and sometimes even returned in favor. What a ride!

Sandra flying in a helicopter for the first time
-Photo courtesy of S. Vandenham

For the Love of the Ocean

Written by Carissa Tetreault

As a sailor, when the alarm sounds it's hard not to think the worse. Your heart pounding, adrenaline rushing, fearing for your life, and the life of your crew. As a sailor, it's your duty to mitigate any threat concerning the safety of the ship to save the life of your crew and to keep your ship afloat.

I have always loved the ocean. There is nothing in the world that compares to seeing nothing but water, breathing air so fresh it feels as if you have never taken a breath before that moment in time. The ocean amazes me. It is mysterious, dangerous, and beautiful. One day you could be sailing on a sea of glass, the next you could be in for the ride of your life. I will never forget the terror and exhilaration of sailing in a regatta.

My passion for going to sea was more than just a need to be close to the ocean. I lived for the smell of the engine room and the sound of the generators as I slept. I have always been a problem solver, driven by the need to fix something. That drive coupled with an aversion to being stuck on deck in the cold and rain, fueled my decision to become a Marine Engineer. I have worked as a Marine Engineer on cruise ships and the Canadian Coast Guard.

My career started shortly after I followed my then boyfriend down to Florida to work on yachts. It wasn't long until I realized I needed a few more qualifications. Not long after I returned home to B.C., my mother received a paper clipping in the mail advertising a new Marine Engineering program at BCIT. I barely blinked before I was polishing up my math in summer school and saving up for college.

The first two years were a jumble of cramming and figuring out who I was as an adult. Looking back, I was so young and completely lost. My career was the only thing that made sense and leaving town for six months to sail on a cruise ship the only thing that made it all worthwhile. I underestimated what it would mean to be a woman undertaking a male-dominated profession. Not only did I have to prove that I could do the job, I had to be tough enough to take a razzing. There were many times I barely knew who I was while trying to fit in.

After completing two sea phases with the Coast Guard, I was finally offered a job with Princess Cruise Lines. The cruise life was an entirely different experience. Many crew members thought of the ship as home, but their home was a traveling vacation spot.

It was the fourth month when the honeymoon effect wore off. I felt like a zombie. We worked four-hours on and eight-hours off every day. My shift at that point was not conducive to getting much shore time, and I was starting to realize that I needed to pursue a different avenue. I had sat down in my cabin for a beer and a Jell-O, one of my go-to meals as I had become sick of the same menu every week on the ship. I turned on the television to zone out before hitting the gym when my TV started to shake. The whole ship was shaking; it took me a moment to remember I was at sea and that we were not having an earthquake. As soon as I realized something was seriously wrong, the engineers call alarm went off. My heart was pounding.

Seconds later, in the control room, I was told there was a crankcase explosion and I thought I was going to be sick to my stomach. I had never been so relieved to be stood down and take off my fire suit. Upon further communications with the engineer on watch, we learned that there was not an explosion. A piston had come through the side of the block and the oil in the air had been so thick that it had resembled smoke. When I checked on the engineer to see if he was okay to continue his watch, he informed me this was nothing compared to the war he'd lived through in his home country. I started to appreciate the need to suit up with my fire team. No matter how much training and practice I had been through, this was real, and I began to appreciate my sheltered life I had growing up when faced with my most terrifying moment on a sound floating ship among other trained sailors ready to fight a fire.

Just three weeks before joining the cruise ship, I met my husband. Three days upon my return we met again, and not too many weeks after that I sent in my resignation. Back to the Coast Guard I went where I have sailed and worked ashore since. Today I have two beautiful little girls and no longer go to sea. I continue to work for the Coast Guard as a Project Technologist. I finally achieved my third-class ticket once I returned from my second maternity leave. I regret, that I am now just short of time to get my second-class ticket. However, I will never take back the decisions I have made to make changes in my career to balance work with my home life. I could not imagine my life without my family. I will allow myself to admit that if I am on one of the ships, or pull out a piece of kit from my sea bag, I still get the pull to go back to sea. This sea story may not be over just yet.

Brianna Snider

Carissa down in the Engine room onboard the CCGS Arrow Post

-Photo courtesy of C. Tetreault

Honeymoon in Alaska

Written by Laureen Bacon

Some things are more than the eye can see, hidden away from the naked eye, and mocking the unsuspecting fool. For us, that is exactly what happened on our way up to Alaska when we quit our jobs and sailed our sailboat called *Blind Date.*

Our first date was a blind date. His mutual friend who was also my sister-in-law, thought we would be perfect together and had set us up to meet. Jacques took me out on his sailboat and we went sailing around Salt Spring Island, one of the Gulf Islands near Victoria. We stayed out past dark and my sister-in-law Mary, who had set us up, was starting to get worried and was wondering if she needed to send the Coast Guard out after us. We had spent the last couple of hours of our first date becalmed in Maple Bay by Duncan, sails luffing, sitting in the cockpit with a glass of wine in hand, and enjoying the conversation. We did have a working motor, but weren't in any hurry to get to shore, we both knew we were destined to be with each other.

A few months later, this all led to trading in the small sailboat for a bigger one, our Catalina 27 called *Blind Date,* to live aboard when we moved to Vancouver. A new boat, new city, new jobs, and a new life. I had never sailed before I met Jacques – everything was so new and exciting, and we decided to get married in December of 1983.

Brianna Snider

My new husband and I decided to take six months off work, take *Blind Date,* and sail her up to Alaska for our honeymoon. Our friends all thought we were crazy for doing it, but we didn't care, we were in love and wanted a proper honeymoon.

After a great deal of preparation on the boat, our friends, who we had met at the marina where we lived, all waved us off as we headed down the Fraser River from Captain Cove Marina, out on a trip of a lifetime up to Alaska. Our good friend Bill Kelly worked for a local newspaper at the time, and took our picture alongside our sailboat before we headed off on our journey and wrote an article about our upcoming adventure. We were famous!

We packed a 20lb. bag of rice, and as many canned goods we could fit without sinking the boat. We even brought our cat Max with us for company. He enjoyed the water and tried to steal scraps of fish whenever he could. Every night that we were tied up along-side in port, he would sneak off into the night only to return in the morning before the fishermen started their day. After a night of being tied up near Nanaimo, B.C. Max still hadn't come home yet, and we weren't sure if he would ever come back to us. We waited it out and stayed an extra day and to our surprise Max came back the very next day. The cat always came back.

On our journey, we fished and threw a crab trap out over the side of the boat almost every night and had fresh fish and crab. We didn't need much to live on and we were both happy in each other's company. We met some amazing boat people on the way and heard all kinds of seafaring stories from local sailors in every port.

On occasion, a cruise ship would pass us by and all we could hear over the loud speaker was "Dinner is served on the lido deck". Sometimes I wished we were about to eat a gourmet meal on one of the cruise ships. But then I thought to myself,

"We are on our own mini cruise ship. Who needs gourmet food when we have all the fresh seafood we want?"

We didn't get as far as we had planned that trip, due to Jacques throwing his back out and having to spend a couple of weeks in Powell River at my sister's home. We arrived in Powell River via the pass between Texada Island and the mainland with the wind behind us, sailing wing-on-wing, with a bow wave threatening to flood the stern. A trip that would normally take the better part of a day only took three hours. I'm sure that was because Jacques was so tense through this ordeal that it was then his back problem occurred.

The farthest town north we sailed to was Ketchikan, Alaska. An amazing little town steeped with history. Ketchikan gets more than 300 days of rain every year, so I'm not sure I could live there but it was neat nonetheless. We had dinner at the fanciest restaurant in town. Our waiter was African-American, and we were chatting, about all the rain the town got. I then made the comment "At least you don't have to worry about getting a tan" before realizing my faux pas.

I held my breath, waiting for his reaction. To my relief, he looked at me, and burst out laughing. Whew! To this day, I'm glad he had a sense of humor.

We then sailed up the Behm Canal a bit farther north. It was such an amazing experience. I've never been to Scandinavia, but this was what I envisioned the fjords to be like - sheer rock walls flanking a narrow inlet. Clouds topped the high cliffs and you could hear the drone of airplanes passing and buzzing overhead. Occasionally, you would get a glimpse of a plane. The only access to the canal is either by boat or plane. Before entering the canal, there is a large bay. There are a few cabins dotted here and there on the shore for people to rent to get the true wild Alaska experience – also only accessible by boat or float plane. In the middle of the bay, there was a very unusual island – a very narrow rock obelisk piercing the sky and covered with vegetation. Very Jurassic.

The time came for us to turn around and head back home. Several times on the way down we had to wait in different ports for the fog to lift. We left Prince Rupert harbor around noon one dreary day after the fog had lifted and proceeded to head south, but just near the mouth of the Skeena River, the wind shifted and blew all the fog back. There happened to be sandbars at the mouth of the river, and our depth sounder was showing less and less water getting shallower by the minute, so we turned and went back the way we came. We spotted a very small island near the mouth of the river, so we motored into the lee of the island, which had deep water close to shore, and dropped an anchor off the bow and the stern so we wouldn't turn on the anchor. We spent the night there, to stay safe from the fog, but with the roar of the river going by, it was difficult to sleep.

As we passed Hole-In-The-Wall near Port Alberni, we encountered a deadhead floating in the water and thought nothing of it. As we slowly moved past the stump to avoid collision we must have disturbed the water with the keel of our boat. Suddenly, that deadhead was no longer a deadhead, but a full-sized tree that shot up out of the water and into the air. There must have been an underwater whirlpool that was sucking the massive tree down and when we disturbed the water, it released it. I don't know who was in awe the most when we saw it happen, Jacques or myself as we both just stared at each other afterwards and were lucky it didn't come crashing down and hit our boat.

After six long months, we returned to our marina and back to reality. We had been in touch with our friends from the marina sporadically while we were away, so they knew what day we would be returning. To our amazement, when we reached Sand Heads at the mouth of the Fraser River in Vancouver, there was a flotilla of boats carrying our friends and waiting to escort us up the river back to our home. We couldn't have asked for a better homecoming from a wonderful adventure at sea.

Picture taken by Bill Kelly in Richmond B.C. in 1983. This was the picture in the newspaper along with the article Bill had wrote. Picture of Jacques and Laureen standing in front of their 27' Catalina Sailboat *Blind Date* about to embark on the journey of a lifetime

-Photo courtesy of L. Bacon

Max attempting to steal some freshly caught fish for dinner

-Photo courtesy of L. Bacon

The Sailor in Me

When I walked into my class for the very first time in sailor school, I was so nervous. I made a point of being early but instead, ended up being right on time for class as I got lost along the way and quickly realized everyone else had shown up early and was sitting down in their seats. At first, I thought I had walked into the wrong classroom because the moment I walked into the room, I had 20 guys staring back at me. I took one large gulp, took a deep breath, and walked chin up into the classroom. There was only one seat left and it just so happened to be right up at the front of the classroom by the instructor.

Everyone turned to look at me as I walked across the front into the classroom and sat down, I could feel the stares I was receiving and suddenly became very self-conscious and aware. They were probably all thinking I was in the wrong classroom too.

"I can do this, I can make it through the first day of school and show these guys I am meant to be here, no fear." I thought to myself.

I managed to make it through the day making a couple of school friends along the way. Our teacher was an old retired sea captain. He had a thick Scottish accent, and grey cap along with a typical sweater vest and looked like the guy from the Highlands fish and chips commercials beard and all. He had amazing knowledge and great sea stories from his days as a sea captain. For some strange reason, he always called everyone Billy. If someone asked a question he always responded, "Aye, Billy".

From the start of my program, I was in constant competition with another guy in the classroom, Jayden, to see who could get the better marks in class. We started off with learning basic knots and hitches and then went on to more complex knots and splices. More in depth than just the basic ones I learned from the Auxiliary Coast Guard. It was so interesting, and the Captain made it fun with hands on learning instead of being in a lecture hall with some 200 other students listening to a prof teach all day. I loved it!

For our practical skills, we went outside a lot. We learned how to throw a heaving line with a Monkey's fist at the end of it and made it into a throwing competition. We had to buy beer for whoever hit the target. Luckily, I was pretty good at throwing a heaving line.

With the Bridge Watchman program, we also learned a lot of nautical terminology. Growing up around boats I knew quite a bit already, but I didn't realize that the nautical language was just that, another language. They have a different name for everything on a boat or a ship. It was neat to think I could speak a secret language.

We learned everything from ships lights, Morse-code, chart work, ship stability, and ship construction. I learned that nautical charts didn't use normal miles they were in nautical miles which is 6082ft. oppose to a regular mile that is only 5280ft.

We went on a lot of field trips to find prospective employers and to learn what it was like to be on some of the different types of boats. We took a tour of the Maritime Museum in Kitsilano and saw the big ship inside that the museum was built around and had been made into a museum. It was the Royal Canadian Mounted police schooner St.Roch. We took a tour of the ship once the museum tour had ended.

Quite often after field trips we would often all end up at a pub, when in sailor school right? Our Captain was usually nice enough to buy us all a round of drinks. It was nice not having to worry about driving in Vancouver. I took the bus everywhere and didn't have to limit my intake. I always made it home safe.

I was doing well in school and loving it, but certain issues were bound to arise. When we were reading a book in class that was written in the 1970's, it listed very clearly as one of the rules: Women were not allowed on board a ship. Of course, I was a little offended and asked myself why they wouldn't change to a more recent book perhaps for school purposes. Meanwhile I was sitting in class in 2006 and you would think in that day in age, women would be more welcomed in a more male dominated workplace. These were just some of the little annoyances I had to deal with being a woman sailor on a regular basis.

I didn't want it to end but knew I had to make money eventually. I was a poor student paying for my apartment in Victoria and paying rent in Vancouver living off a minimal income at a lower paying job. I had a looming student loan and needed a good job, maybe a pension, and medical benefits too. I needed to make it in the real world and get a "grown up" job.

The final exam consisted of 100 multiple choice questions. I was one of the last people to finish writing my exam but later found out I had one of the top three marks out of 20 people. I was ecstatic! I had made it, the only girl in the class. I had shown everyone I could do it, I was finally finished my schooling, and could move on to bigger and better things. I had bigger fish to fry so to speak. On my last day of my MED B2 course (firefighting), I received a phone call while I was sitting in class from the Human Resources department at the Coast Guard. I had already put in my application before I left for school and they wanted me to start working in two weeks' time. I was beyond thrilled. After I hung up the phone I started jumping up and down like a crazy person, and everyone in the class probably thought I was fending off a bee or something. This was it, what I had trained to do. I somehow had managed to meet my career goal in life. It felt so surreal, I didn't know what to think. I had never worked on a ship before and here I was starting in two weeks' time. I had to go to the office to pick up my uniform, sign forms, and get a list of things I needed to bring with me to sea. I wanted to be prepared, but nothing could have prepared me for what was to come on my first day of work on the ship.

On top of the Great Wall of China

Story by Michelle Gendron

Sailing, can lead you to travel unknown destinations, take you on adventures, and see different parts of the world. You never know where you will end up.

As a nomadic girl from Victoria, B.C., I have always dreamed of travelling the world. Little did I know my career as a sailor would soon take me to 25 different countries during the three months when I signed up to work on a cruise ship. I worked for Princess Cruise lines as a bar manager and managed about 60 staff members on board. The cruise ship line was based out of Australia and cruised to destinations like Australia, South Africa, India, Korea, Japan, Indonesia, and China.

The cruise line paid for my ticket to fly to Australia where I was to meet and board the ship. The company gave me a week's notice before I was to leave my home in Victoria to start my new and exciting job, and I had no idea what to expect. Unfortunately for me, as a young, Caucasian, Canadian female on board a cruise ship, I was pigeonholed from the moment I stepped onboard the ship. I walked into a managerial position at age 27 and had more seniority than some people who had been working their way up the ladder for the last 15-20 years. Several of my peers and co-workers resented me for it, which made it much more difficult to do my job on the ship.

The two people who harassed me the most over this were the two bosses directly above my position. They tortured me every day, telling me I couldn't do my job and that I didn't deserve to be there. They were the reason I cut my patrol short and left after only three months at sea. For the most part, the rest of my crew was amazing. They were made up of all different cultures including Filipino, East Indian from India, European, and North American. Most of the people I was responsible for, working as the bar manager, were Filipino. It was sweet because most of them called me ma'am even though they were old enough to be my father, I had tattoos that were visible, and it looked like I had just graduated high school. That made me a little bit uncomfortable but after a little bit of coaxing, they started saying Michelle and then whisper under their breath "ma'am".

I met many different people on board the cruise ship, some of whom were crew and some passengers. I was first introduced to Adrian by a fellow crew member. He was a big Croatian fellow with a thick accent and I later found out he was the Chief Engineer of the cruise ship. For those of you who don't know the hierarchy on a ship, the Chief Engineer is the second highest position besides a Captain. He controls the entire Engine Room crew from Officers to Oilers. Everyone respected him and was even a bit afraid of him but as I got to know him better, I found out he was a big teddy bear. I was unaware that my friend who had introduced us had "warned" him that I was a lesbian. I had no idea that it would even be an issue but apparently in Croatia, it's not uncommon to still be violent towards gays and lesbians and even throw food and stones at them. I was appalled when I first found out, but as I gradually got to hang out with Adrian more and drank with him at the bar it was water under the bridge. I just couldn't believe that some countries and some religions were that against my sexual orientation when it is

35

so accepted in Canada in general. It was quite funny how many different guys hit on me and expected me to sleep with them on the ship not knowing that my preference was women.

I had always wanted to travel the world but when I signed up to work on a cruise ship I never dreamed of some of the places I would end up. I travelled to places like South Africa and India, but my most favorite place of all was China. I had always wanted to go there, and most of all I wanted to see the Great Wall. I was lucky in that I ended up having an entire day off while we were in China, so a friend of mine came along and we both went to see the extraordinary site. When we got there, it was as far as the eye could see. As I was climbing the stairs I thought to myself, "This is really happening". It was a beautiful site at the top of the wall. In my mind, I was experiencing "pure bliss" or whatever that may be. There were vendors selling trinkets along the top of the wall and in some areas, the wall was only a few feet across. Someone with a fear of heights may not want to put this on their bucket list but it was one of the most amazing days of my life and I owe it all to working onboard a cruise ship and travelling the world.

I don't regret ever going, and I would go back in a heartbeat, but I would work in a different department. For someone looking for adventure, who wants to see the world on a budget, and become a sailor, cruise ships are the way to go. For me, I could achieve my lifetime goal and crossed another one off my bucket list.

Fire in the Hole!

Written by Molly Peterson

The importance of boat and fire drill exercises are often taken for granted. If something were to happen out at sea, you want to ensure you have the proper training and knowledge about what to do in case of an emergency.

Well, where to start? I work as a junior mate in marine shipping on the Great Lakes. Working on the Great Lakes is very different than working on the ocean. Everything from the words we call things, to the way we do the same job. I've worked with men who had previously worked on ocean going vessels (we call them "salties" on the lakes) and they found the way we did certain things was very old fashioned, more laid back, and less prim and proper. The way of life on the Great Lakes is so different from working on ocean voyages.

I started school and joined my first ship two years ago, when I was just 17. I am a big city girl, but I don't mind getting my hands dirty. I have been told I am very easy to get along with which makes it easier for me to ask things of others. People don't usually give me grief about asking them to do something. I am always willing to learn and if someone is trying to help me, I always listen to what they say. I always try to laugh and crack jokes, because I figure if you're going to be on a ship for months on end you should have a good time with it. I had a non-conventional childhood, so you could say I am used to being away from my home and family for long periods of time, which does make this job a bit easier.

Brianna Snider

I handle all kinds of bulk cargoes, but once I get a higher ticket I want to move up into the world of Dynamic Positioning. I have only been out to sea for two seasons, but already I know that I love it and can't wait to make a full career out of it. When I was young I learned about the marine industry through my uncle. He told me what his job entailed, and I was amazed. At 12 years old, I joined the Royal Canadian Sea Cadets and discovered how much I loved being on the water as much as the other aspects of shipboard life. I love how free I felt gliding through the water with the wind blowing through my hair.

My favorite part of working on the ship, are the amazing sights I get to see and the people I get to meet. Every night I get to watch the sun set over the horizon, it's different and seemingly more beautiful every time. Some of my favorite times have been in the middle of the lake when you can't see any land around. It's such a calming feeling to look over the water and not worry about any other distractions; it's just the water and me.

Being a woman in a male dominated industry can have its trials and tribulations though. Most of the younger sailors are very kind and helpful but some sailors who have been around for many years are still set in their ways. It used to be considered bad luck for there to be a female onboard the ship, and some of the older men still believe that. I've realized that there is always going to be a least one grumpy man on board any ship who brings down the moral of the crew, the only thing to do is just keep your head up and do your job to the very best of your abilities.

In the old days, people worked their way up through the ranks to become an officer or captain. They would start at the bottom as a deckhand or wheelsman for a few years then study like crazy before taking their exams to get an officer's ticket. Nowadays, most officers go through a cadet program which fast-tracks that process considerably. This program consists of four years of post-secondary education during which time there are school terms and sea phase terms. The number of sea phase terms varies depending on the school, but each cadet must have at least 12 months sea time before they can write their exams. I am currently half way through my sea time and I am exactly on schedule to have it all finished in time to write my exams.

My main duty onboard is the safety of the ship. I keep a safe watch while the ship is underway, following all rules and regulations of safe navigation; when we are in port, I help make sure that all loading and unloading operations are going well as per the Chief-Mate's plan.

On the ship I was sailing on, we often had issues with our 45-year-old engines. The fuel injectors are continuously melting and wearing away. One trip as we were sailing through the New York section of the St Lawrence Seaway, the port fuel lines broke and started spraying hot fuel on the starboard engine. The entire engine room filled with smoke and the ship's general alarm was sounded. Once everyone was mustered and accounted for, men were suited up while all the vents were closed, and the fixed CO2 system was prepared in case it had to be deployed. Life rafts were prepared, which is routine for emergencies. The first team of men went down and got the fire out quickly. Luckily it caused minimal damage to the equipment other than the starboard engine. I have never seen people move as quickly as I did that morning. 60-year-old men who usually shuffle across the deck were running to get to their muster station. Thanks to all the regular boat and fire drills we have, everyone stayed calm and collected and knew what their job was. Once the fire was extinguished, we had to report it to vessel traffic services as well as the American Coast Guard since we were in American waters. It all happened so quickly that when it was all over I had to step back and think of what had just happened. A normal day on the river could have been a catastrophe if it hadn't been for all our training. I remain very grateful for that.

I must say the scariest thing that happened to me while working at sea was a medical emergency we had onboard the ship. The chief mate and the second mate were good friends and hung out at home all the time. On this occasion, the chief mate walked into the second-mate's cabin and found him lying on the floor unconscious and barely breathing. Luckily, we were in port at the time and paramedics were called. He stopped breathing twice while the paramedics were trying to prepare him for transport and they had to do CPR to keep him alive. The second mate is a very tall muscular man and we had a very difficult time trying to get him outside so that he could be lifted off the ship. We finally got him out on deck and had to use the prevision hoist to get him on the ground. It took over an hour from the time he was found to the time the ambulance left. We were told he stopped breathing again on the way to the hospital. If he had been found even five minutes later or had been away at sea, he probably wouldn't have survived the whole ordeal. We later found out he was taking pills from a recent surgery along with supplements for working out and he was putting too much pressure on his heart and lungs. That gave me a whole new perspective, and made me appreciate the good health I might otherwise take for granted. It also put into perspective the difficulties working onboard a ship being in tight quarters all the time.

Being a woman onboard can be challenging. Trying to get men to take you seriously can be the biggest challenge. Lots of these men still have it in their minds that women are inferior to men, which can make being a female officer a struggle. It can also be difficult for people who are very close with their family. Being away from home for long periods of time can take a toll on relationships and family life. I am single and still young, nor do I plan to settle down until I can really commit myself. I do get homesick sometimes after being away for a few months, but I just think to myself that it will all be worth it in the long run when I'm living my dreams. Since I am trying to get all my sea time, so I can write my exams, I usually stay out for as long as possible before going home. Many companies put in place regulations for a maximum amount of time you can be onboard before you must go home. With my current company, I stay out for the full time-allowed: four and a half months. Once I get my ticket I will have more options for when I want to go home.

This industry requires very thick skin. Some old school people will try to break you, and you must prove to them that you can handle it. I can honestly say that I've never been through emotional or physical harassment, but I can also say that I have been through some sexual harassment. The worst part of that, in my experience, is when it's the Captain who is doing it. Many times, I've been asked inappropriate questions about my personal life or had my personal space invaded. Unfortunately, some women come onboard the ship looking to have some fun with the men, which leads the men to generalize that any women can be an easy sexual target. It does make me uncomfortable, but I've learned to let the person know that his contact or attention is unwelcome. Usually, this puts an end to it, right then and there.

Fortunately, on the ships I've been on I have always had my own cabin and private bathroom. Most crew members get their own room, but many ships still have communal bathrooms. If I were to have to share, it would have to be with another female. On the first ship I was on, both the cooks were female, and we often had female relief mates, but I have also been on ships where I was the only woman on board. I haven't found that women need to work harder than men. Regardless of your gender, you're expected to do your job to the best of your abilities. That's all anyone can do. Everybody makes mistakes; the trick is to learn from them.

Before going to sea, I expected it to be very difficult for women. I have since found that it's not as bad as I had thought it might be. I have been lucky with the crews that I've worked with; I've had a very positive experience so far. I encourage women to get into this industry, or any trade, because it is a rewarding career. That said, I do warn that thick skin is required. You must be able to hold your own and still be fair to everybody. As for making a life and career at sea, I couldn't picture myself doing anything else!

Molly on the deck of a container ship on one of the Great Lakes

-Photo courtesy of M. Peterson

Don't Miss the Boat

Story by Channah Samuels

If you are not back on the ship when it's supposed to leave it will leave without you. For every minute, a cruise ship wastes staying tied up when departing for the next leg of the trip, it costs them approximately $800 (CAN) per minute of lost revenue.

While working and living in the Philippines, a friend of mine wanted to leave the Philippines and get a job working for a cruise ship line.

She asked if I could go with her for support and I said, "sure, why not?"

We went to the office in Manila and handed in our resumes. Those chosen, would fly to England for training and leave in a weeks' time. I applied to support my friend but as it turned out, I was chosen, and she wasn't. I felt bad for her, but I wanted to go. I had always wanted to travel and see the world. The pay was also almost eight times what I could make in the Philippines and I could save up for a house.

So, there I was ready to get on a plane to England where I would do eight weeks of training. I was going to be training as an Esthetician, so I could work in the spa on the ship doing manicures, pedicures, and facial treatments, etc.

I met my now husband working on board the ship during my second patrol. Each patrol was about eight months long. I was lucky because I was classified as staff instead of crew, so I had access to the crew decks and the passenger decks, and could use all the amenities I wanted. I could also leave the ship and go exploring whenever the ship was in port as the spa was closed when we were tied alongside. I had a little bit more "free" time then some of the crew members did and could go on day excursions when tied up in different countries.

I met my husband Dave for the first time and he fell in love with me right then and there. He was a Canadian man who lived in Victoria, B.C. I didn't know it at the time, but later after we married I left the Philippines and we ended up moving to Victoria and having a son together. Before I met my husband however, I paid to have a house built for my parents back in the Philippines. Even though I was only making the equivalent of about $1500 a month Canadian, that was more than enough to live very well in the Philippines. For the number of hours, you work on board a cruise ship that relates to about $3 an hour working 10-12 hours a day. Again, this was much more money than I would have made back home.

One trip when we were tied up alongside in Victoria, B.C., my fiancé at the time now my husband, wanted me to meet his family and have lunch with them. We took our laundry bags with us ashore to clean our dirty laundry and off we went. I thought we needed to be back to the ship at 18:00. We arrived at Ogden Point at the cruise ship terminal just before 17:00 when suddenly, we heard the ships horn blast signaling it was about to leave port. We started running as fast as our legs would carry us to climb onboard the ship. Dave and I were hand in hand, laundry bags in our other hands running as fast as we could back to our ship as we heard the blasting sound of the ships horn yet again. We must have got the time mixed up.

"I thought we were supposed to be back at the ship at 18:00 not 17:00" Dave asked?

Lucky for us my friend Sarah told the ship's Captain we were on our way, and that we wouldn't just "jump ship".

Dave and I, arrived just in the nick of time with only minutes to spare. They didn't look too pleased when we finally arrived on the ship.

We were both called to the bridge to speak with the Captain immediately after we boarded. I was quite nervous as I had never actually met the Captain and I knew we were in trouble. I didn't know what he was going to say to us.

I thought to myself, "This is it, we are both going to lose our jobs on the spot."

We were standing in front of the Captain and I was expecting him to reprimand us. He told us not to be late again and then he started talking about his wife who was standing beside him and how she was up on the bridge visiting. I mentioned that I liked his wife's hat and we started talking and laughing away having a great conversation.

My husband and I both left the bridge that day with new friends. We weren't in trouble at all and the ship departed right on schedule.

The Captain was sure to add before we left that we were not to be late returning to the ship again. (We were supposed to be back half an hour prior to sailing)

"Yes Sir!" we both chimed in. A sailor never misses the boat!

Channah loving her career at sea

-Photo courtesy of C. Samuels

Channah on top of the world

-Photo courtesy of C. Samuels

In the Engine room

Written by Louise-Anne Granger

I was an Engineer in the Canadian Coast Guard fleet. My first ship after graduation from the college was a medium sized Coast Guard vessel, a buoy tender. The engine room crew consisted of five engineers: a chief, senior, day worker, and two watch keepers. There were also three oilers, one on each watch and a day working oiler. We were a tight-knit crew and I have fond memories of sailing back then.

We had a female oiler on the crew. She and I probably set a Canadian record, if not a world record when we ended up on the same engineering watch together! The chief, seeing our conspiring looks and giggles, first wondered if he had made a good decision in putting us on the same watch. However, we must have done well as we shared the same watch a few times after that.

One midnight to noon watch, I was doing work on the oily water separator. The oily water separator removes oil from water, sending the oil to a retention tank to dispose of later and sending the clean water overboard. The separator was installed on top of the ship's frames in the engine room. This forms a space where there is no tank top between the vertical edge of the double bottom and the ship's side. This area is called the bilge; water and leaking oil accumulate in this area. It can become quite the smelly soup from a collection of different liquids.

While working on the separator, I dropped a combination wrench about six inches long in an awkward spot in the bilge. Being new to the ship, I felt bad about having lost a wrench, so I decided to go fishing for it. I grabbed the magnet on a stick and started poking around. The magnet stuck to the hull at every dip until I felt something different. I pulled the magnet out of the bilge water and the wrench attached at the end of it was about 15 inches long! I don't know what was in that bilge water, but it did an impressive job with the wrench. Something that was in the "smelly soup" made it all shiny and clean.

Of course, this was a different wrench than the one I had dropped, and I kept looking until I found the wrench I had lost. Obviously, whoever had dropped the larger wrench didn't feel as bad as I did and did not bother getting it back. Could this be a difference between a man's and a woman's work ethic?

When I first joined that ship, I inspected every nook and cranny as part of my due diligence routine. There was an electrical panel behind the switchboard in the engine control room and when I opened the door to see what circuits the panel supplied, I discovered a picture of a scantily clad woman. I smiled and closed the door. A few months later, when it was myself and the woman oiler working together again, my watch partner got hold of a Chippendale calendar and we hung it in the control room. When we came down for our next watch, the men had defaced the calendar, cutting and pasting the models in suggestive positions!

I thought to myself, "If they can put up pictures of naked girls, we should be able to do the same."

I have never been on a ship that didn't have a woman onboard, however, I have been the only woman among 13 men. Having women onboard certainly helped everyone get home after one trip. We were crew changing out of Sandspit and the crew coming to relieve us were all men. When the plane's crew did their pre-departure calculations after we checked our entire luggage, the take-off weight was going to be too high. Thankfully, they had done their calculations using the weight for all male passengers. They recalculated considering that there were two women on board the plane and we were then cleared for take-off. I think it should still have been touch and go as I was carrying more weight that I should have in my luggage and the other woman was taller than average. However, we all made it home safe and sound!

I have now been working ashore for nearly as long as I went to sea. I still miss going to sea. The camaraderie and work ambiance are so different from working in an office atmosphere. Who can complain about a two-minute commute to work from your bed to your watch and getting to eat three squares a day from your fabulous cook onboard! Those were the days and I will never forget them.

Victoria Coast Guard Base in Victoria, B.C.

-Photo courtesy of B. Snider

To Pee or Not to Pee

Being a woman sailor on a ship full of men has its perks. Firstly, they are sometimes nice to look at, and secondly, they usually treat you like royalty if you are the only woman onboard.

The not so perky side to being on a ship full of men when you are one of the only woman sailors is that using the "heads" can become a tricky business. On my first patrol at sea, all the crew members had to share the same three-stall bathroom. This was exceptionally unfortunate should the guy next to you have had chili or something similar for dinner earlier that evening. It was also unfortunate when you really had to go, and you didn't want anyone to hear you pee (or go number two), so you had to wait until the entire bathroom cleared out. This was also a problem when someone was seasick and had to chuck their cookies in the bathroom. Who really wants the guy next to you listening to that? Women don't always fart rainbows and butterflies, but that's not to say we want men to know the finer details of our flatulence.

There was also no such thing as a sanitary disposal bin onboard the ship, so it was extremely hard when it was your time of the month to dispose of sanitary waste. Quite often I would resort to stuffing tampons up my sleeve when heading to the bathroom and discarding them in the regular garbage. The only problem with the regular garbage was the ship used clear plastic garbage bags and so anytime someone emptied the garbage, it was displayed for everyone to see. When there are only a couple of women onboard the vessel, it isn't hard to decipher to whom the tampons in the trash belonged. How embarrassing.

It was different sharing accommodation with the crew since they were almost all men. Sometimes we even had to share cabins, although we would be on opposite watches. For instance, if I was working midnight to noon, my cabin mate would work noon to midnight, so we were never in the cabin at the same time. I just had to share the messy cabin with a stinky boy. A little baby powder in the work boots never hurt anyone.

The most amusing part of my day was when there were a few guys hanging around after I had a shower. I don't know what they were expecting to see, but maybe they thought they were going to sneak a peek or something. I don't know. After all, these sailors go to sea for a month at a time and don't have any women to look at besides you or the few other women on board. I guess I don't blame them, but it was still one of those annoyances that I couldn't escape.

My first patrol at sea I worked 12-hours on 12-hours off for 28 days in a row. It was a pretty good deal, giving me a month off at a time. During that time, if I wanted, I could travel and go on an adventure somewhere down in the tropics, or I could stay at home and hang out with family and friends. The only drawback was that I had to be away from my family and friends for a month, sometimes longer, which could prove difficult. Missing birthdays, anniversaries, and sometimes even Christmas and New Year's, was hard. The real kicker was when friends and family started having babies and I couldn't be there for the births, or came home to a three or four-week old baby. I felt like I always missed out on something.

When I first arrived at the ship I really didn't know what to expect. I slowly walked up the steep gangway and made my way on to the deck. I was first introduced to the boatswain (my immediate boss on deck) and a couple of the other seamen. I was shown where I could put my sea bag and where my cabin was and then we all met back on the deck to start work.

Everyone could tell I was a greenhorn right away. I guess my steel-toed boots, crisp clean uniform, and clean hands gave me away. My boots were so shiny and new, they stuck out like a sore thumb. They had yet to see a speck of dirt, but it didn't take long before they were covered in paint, buoy slim, grease, and sea salt. My uniform still had creases on it and my hands had yet to get dirty. That would soon change.

The first thing we did was a familiarization of the ship because I was brand new. There were two other deckhands that were brand new and that had never been on a ship before too so we all went along with one of the lead hands and he gave us the grand tour.

I'd never been on a large steel ship before. I felt like a tiny ant exploring the great outdoors. We went over all the emergency procedures and where all the muster stations were. A muster station is where you go in case of emergency to gear up (depending on the emergency) and to be instructed to abandon ship if need be. All the muster stations have life rafts available, as well as immersion suits to keep you warm. There is also one muster station at a lifeboat, which would tow all the life rafts to safety in an emergency. In case of a fire on board the ship, you would suit up in turn out gear (firefighting gear) in your designated fire party and go fight the fire. Unfortunately, when it comes to a ship, if something bad like that happens you have no choice but to try and tackle it to save the ship. It's just you, the large steel hull, and the water below, and you hope that the steel hull stays afloat or else you are all in trouble.

We were given a tour of the bridge. I had never been on a real bridge before and the closest thing to it was a simulator I tried while attending sailor school. There were so many electronics and charts, and so many flashing buttons to push. It was a little overwhelming at a first glance.

Women at Sea

On the ship I was on, I learned there were 24 crewmembers on board of which there were only four women: two-seamen (including myself), the second mate, and the Captain were all women. Not a very high ratio but higher than most vessels I later learned. I should also mention that the Captain was the only female Captain in the fleet at the time. So, it was rare to see and amazing to meet such a profound, brilliant woman in such a powerhouse position. I look up to her to this date.

After the tour, I was put to work doing a lot of chipping, painting, and grinding.

"I'm supposed to do what now?" I thought to myself.

I thought being a sailor was training for search and rescue, tying knots, steering the ship, and being a look out. I didn't know how to use power tools or paint. I'd never even really used a wrench before. I began to wonder what I'd got myself into.

I learned quickly that there are many different types of vessels. Here are some to name a few:

- Ice Breakers
- Search and Rescue Vessels
- Buoy tenders
- Tug boats
- Fishing Vessels/Crabbing/Prawning
- Cruise Ships
- Deep Sea Vessels (Cargo/Freighter)
- Sailing Vessel
- Ferries
- Cable Ships
- Science Vessels
- Submarines
- Warships (Frigates, Destroyers)
- Dive Boats
- Aircraft Carriers
- Self-righting vessels

Brianna Snider

- ⚓ RHIBs
- ⚓ Pilot Boats

The boatswain was a good teacher. He taught me how to use all the tools and what they were called. That's right, I didn't even know the names of half the tools in the ship's workshop. I was used to working with phones and computers, not power tools and paint brushes.

All the other deckhands were kind and helped me along the way. Most of the time, I felt like a lost little puppy just following everyone else around the ship. The other female deckhand had been around for a while, so she showed me the ropes (literally) quite a bit too.

I still felt like a fish out of water, but I was slowly getting used to the idea of being a deckhand. For the first two weeks, all I did was paint and grind the rust out of the ship's deck. I'd never done so much grunt work before in my entire life. All those times I thought high school was tough, or that working in the fast food industry was gross, couldn't begin to prepare me for what lay ahead on my journey to become a sailor.

The food was great. We had two cooks on board and one steward, so we were well looked after. I'd never eaten such gourmet food. Sorry mom! After every meal, there was always a dessert to follow. Of course, I had to try everything! I was wondering how on earth the crew on board could keep their slim figure with desserts always around, but I guess the 12-hour days you put in of hard work every day paid off.

I became a quartermaster, so I was going to be working midnight to noon with a watch partner. Little did I know I was meeting my future husband at the time.

The first thing I noticed when I met Blaine for the first time was his gorgeous baby blue eyes. They were so kind, warm, and welcoming. He was one of the only guys on the ship who didn't look at me like I was a piece of meat. Probably because

Women at Sea

he was married, but we still became extremely good friends. You really get to know a lot about someone working alongside them 12-hours a day every day for a month.

We became friends and his marriage was short lived. I helped him through the tough times of divorce and was who he turned to when he needed someone to listen. Little did I know that a year and a half later I would finally cave after he asked me out several times, and never look back.

Blaine taught me many things, like how we had to take the garbage and recycling out every night and do our routine cleaning stations. Quartermasters keep the ship tidy as well as steer the ship when everyone else is in bed. We were the elves in the middle of the night watching over everyone as they slept, cleaning as we wandered the empty alley ways.

I had to learn everything quickly, and although my school had taught me a great deal, learning something in a classroom is completely different from doing it in real life. That was the hard part, taking everything, I had in my head and putting it to good use.

Having never actually steered a real ship before, I was extremely nervous; it was a big ship and I didn't want to crash. Boy would I be embarrassed!

Day by day, I was learning new things trying to cram everything into my head, so I would remember it all. Blaine was a huge help and guided me through. Finally, we were off to sea!

We worked for a few days, jumping from ship to workboat to land, taking supplies ashore. It was hard work being at sea, and it was just the start. My hair was a mess, my nails had dirt and grime under them, and even after I washed them they were still dirty. My work boots stunk to high heavens and my feet looked like they needed a good scrub and a pedicure. I don't think I had ever worked so hard in my life.

We did helicopter operations at many different lighthouses. That was probably one of my favorite things to do. I literally stood 30 feet below the helicopter as it took items off the ship and headed for shore. I would often think to myself, "I love my job."

It just so happened we were right around the area called Hot Springs Cove. We ended up sending the RHIB out so everyone off watch could go to the hot springs. Since I was off at noon for the day, we could enjoy a refreshing drink in the hot springs, relaxing into the afternoon sun on the west coast of Vancouver Island, with great company and an amazing view.

A beautiful sunset tied up in port at Patricia Bay, Sidney. Photo taken from Monkey's Island on top of the bridge.

-Photo courtesy of B Snider

Bioluminescence

Story by Vanessa Downie

Your mental well being should be taken seriously. When you are not in the right state of mind it is hard to focus and do your job properly, and sometimes you can even become agitated, or upset for no good reason. As sailors, we must take care of our selves.

We were sailing around Vancouver Island; there was not a cloud in sight. After dark, I could see the twinkling lights of the stars were reflecting and glimmering on top of the glassy surface of the ocean. As I looked down, I could see the wonderful colors of the bioluminescence. This happened to be my favorite experience out at sea. I was born in Nanaimo, B.C. but my parents up rooted me to live in Edmonton, where I grew up. I missed the ocean and always had a special connection to the it. Therefore, I choose a career in the Navy and chose to become a sailor at sea.

As a Naval Communicator, I did my basic training and then was sent off to do a three-month communicator course where I learned to talk on a VHF and take and record messages. I learned how to watch for distress signals like solar flares and SOS messages. Three weeks after I finished my course, they asked what I was doing and if I was available to travel. They wanted me to go down to Panama and do an anti-narcotics patrol looking for suspicious vessels. I jumped on the opportunity to travel and that first patrol was where I met my fiancé, Josh. At the time, my aunt and uncle were living in Panama and I figured I would go and visit them while I was there. I brought Josh even though we weren't dating yet at the time, and apparently my aunt and uncle knew we were destined for each other before we did. After that patrol, we were no longer allowed to work together as we worked in the same department and he was my superior officer. He later got posted ashore and I continued to go to sea for the time being.

Sailing with the navy has its ups and downs. My breaking point was when I had had an unusually bad day. I came back to my bunk to find that one of my two pillows were missing. We were all assigned a pillow, but I had brought my own pillow from home and liked sleeping with two pillows.

When I saw that it was gone I said, "They've taken everything from me and now they've taken my pillow!"

In that instance, I just wanted to go home. Tears streamed down my face and I began wallowing in self-pity. Just then I looked down to see someone had moved my pillow onto the bottom bunk. I had burst into tears over nothing, but sometimes I just needed a good cry to let it all out. This was especially true when I felt misunderstood or judged.

I always tried my best to be kind to my fellow sailor on board and tried to help everyone out when I could. However, I didn't quite feel like it was widely reciprocated across the ship. People didn't go out of their way to help others, and I found that troubling. I remember one particularly emotional patrol on our way back from Hawaii; I was battling a nervous disorder and coming off my medication. While in Hawaii I had bought a bunch of wrapped chocolates and placed one neatly on every woman sailor's pillow as a thank you for her support. Along with the chocolate was a little note saying what I admired about each woman as a little pick me up. Afterwards, most of them couldn't believe I would go out of my way to make such a sweet gesture. Maybe that's what the ship needed a little bit more of. I was one woman out of about 30 onboard the vessel. The crew was over 230 people, so we were still classified as a minority. Maybe the ship needed more women to have more of a "woman's touch" onboard. It may have made life a bit easier for everyone.

One day a male co-worker wanted to play hockey when we were tied up alongside in Victoria and I said, "Go for it! I'll cover your shift". People were in awe that I did this and couldn't really understand what compelled me to do it. I just knew that if the roles were reversed, I would want someone to cover for me. That kind of give-and-take needed to happen more onboard the ship.

I was in awe of the raw beauty of life at sea. It was so powerful and magnificent. It felt surreal sailing through the water on a flat calm day, not a cloud in the sky, the water was shimmering with bioluminescence; it truly felt like we were sailing through the heavens. I will always remember that part of going to sea. Days like that kept me going back to sea. It made it all worthwhile, even when I got seasick on occasion or was harassed or razzed on.

I would certainly recommend the sailor life to other women to try. The only drawback working for the Navy would be when you ever decide to have a family, the moment you become pregnant they take you off the ship, for your own safety and for the baby's safety. After we get married, my fiancé and I will probably want to start a family of our own. When that happens, my life and career at sea will be over. It is hard to have to choose between your dream job and a family, but I know that those who have kids and sail are unhappy being away from them, and those who don't have kids are happy being at sea. It is a sacrifice a woman must make.

Sailing is a part of me, and I am happy to have had a chance to sail. I never would have met my husband if I hadn't gone to sea. I will continue to help my fellow man and hope to pursue a career as a nurse once my contract is up in the Navy. One thing I would have to say to anyone thinking about a career at sea would be this: know who you are before you begin. Know your morals, know your standards, know who you are inside and don't change who you are just because everyone else swears or tells crude jokes. Happy sailing!

Abandon Ship

Story by Stacey Aikers

As a sailor always working on the water, you always run the risk of your vessel sinking. You hope and pray that if something happens someone will come to your rescue or that you are close enough to shore to make it to safety. Nothing you do or train for can truly ever prepare you for a real-life emergency, and nothing can prepare you for the harsh conditions of the west coast.

Even though my father was in the Navy, I never planned to work on the ocean. It happened by accident. When I was little, my father was an Engineer in the Navy and we were always moving around. He bought a fishing boat, so I started fishing at a young age. We later moved from Sooke to Singapore, but we were never far away from the ocean.

In 1979, my boyfriend at the time wanted me to go out with him on a fishing vessel. I jumped at the opportunity, quit my job at a bank, and the rest is history. I went out on a three-man boat going halibut fishing all over the west coast and up in the Queen Charlotte Islands. The fishing boat at the time had recently lost its crew after the owner's truck was stolen, totaled, and the delinquent crew members were fired. The owner then came to my boyfriend and asked me if I could work for him and be the ship's cook. I gave my consent, and jumped ship.

Never in my life had I cooked for others before becoming a cook on a ship. On my first trip on a fishing vessel, the first thing I did when I boarded the ship was call my mother to ask her why she had never taught me how to cook. My first meal I had to prepare for the crew was breakfast. I made scrambled eggs and cooked the full dozen. The Captain came by, scooped all the eggs from the pan and asked where the food for the other crew members was. He ate all 12 scrambled eggs I had cooked. I can only imagine the look on my face of utter disbelief as he rushed off. I often referred to the *Joy of Cooking* for tips and recipes but never followed the recipes. I had to adjust to the crew's likes and dislikes, all the while coming up with new ways to impress them and their empty bellies.

I learned quickly how to calculate and prepare meals, so I had enough food and served every meal on time. I have never been late for a meal yet. During my everyday routine, I wake up every morning at 4:30 am to start breakfast, leave time to clean up, then immediately I'm on to the next meal. I manage to bake cookies or muffins in between for snacks and break time for the hungry fishermen.

The men on the ship quickly came to see me as a mother figure as I was the only woman onboard the ship. I was affectionately referred to as the "mother hen". Halfway through a patrol, some of them would accidentally slip up and call me "mom". I didn't mind.

In the early days, I usually shared a cabin with the men. I didn't mind so much as I always wore clothes to bed and they were always very respectful. One of the boats I was on had a shower on the back deck with a little curtain and it was the only way we could have a hot shower, but of course on windy days the curtain would fly out exposing my bare butt to the elements. For this reason, I had to make sure none of the other crew members were around watching me take a shower.

In 1985, I was sailing on a 70-ft. wooden seine fishing boat with six crew members onboard when we became shipwrecked. The ship was called the Corina No.1 and I was the only woman onboard. The weather was snotty, tossing waves like a toddler amid a tantrum with the wind blowing the tiny boat all over the place. We were just off the coast of Port Renfrew when we were at anchor and we started dragging anchor at about 3:00am in the morning. The anchor chain whipped around and tore the wheel completely off the helm. We started drifting quickly towards shore getting caught in the waves and ended up on the rocks nearby.

The Captain cried, "Mayday, mayday, mayday" into the VHF.

The rescue coordination center asked where we were, and he replied, "I don't know where we are. If I knew where we were, we wouldn't be lost, grounded, and sinking."

The Captain then yelled to the crew, "Get your survival suits on!"

The suits were not where they were supposed to be, so I began frantically searching for them. Two men tried to light an emergency flare, but it sizzled hopelessly across the deck. Nothing was going according to plan and I couldn't help but wonder if we were going to make it out alive. The lifeboat that I personally picked up from Mustang didn't inflate. We were out of luck and running out of time. We knew there was no choice but to abandon ship. We all hit the icy cold water of the Pacific Ocean as the ship was swiftly sinking beside us. We had to help our Captain swim to shore, as he didn't know how to swim. Not many captains do. *"Why bother trying to fight the sea when the sea will swallow you anyways?"* So, the saying goes.

Once ashore, we waited for the Coast Guard, but they couldn't come to our rescue because the weather conditions were so bad. The helicopter couldn't fly, and their RHIBs couldn't get to us onshore because the waves were too high, and it was way too dangerous for them. I was thankful we were close enough to be able to swim to shore or our crew would have been engulfed by the sea. Feeling like drowned rats and coming to terms with what had just happened, all six of us made it safely to shore. We were picked up by locals living in the area who took us to Port Renfrew where we all took a taxi cab back to Victoria. We stayed at the Red Lion Hotel in Victoria and flew home the next day. We were so lucky to survive that ordeal but after a few days at home I would go to grab one of my personal belongings and I would realize it was gone. Everything I had brought with me on that fishing trip was, at the bottom of the ocean. I barely grabbed enough clothes to escape; all I had were the clothes that I was wearing. It was so surreal, and I will never forget that feeling of utter disbelief. We were all so lucky to escape death.

Working at sea can be challenging but I am still glad I chose a life at sea. I love going away and I love my free time at home. I work 18-hour days, but I always get a month off where I can go traveling or whatever I may choose. It's easy for me to go away because I enjoy the lifestyle but it's always hard on my grown kids. My daughter still cries every time I leave as she knows the all too real dangers of working at sea. For now, I will continue working on boats perhaps until my days of retirement. Working at sea will always be a part of me and as much as it may try, this job will never bring me down.

Women at Sea

The Corrina No.1 up on the rocks and sinking off the West Coast of Vancouver Island.

-Photo taken by Alan Haig Brown courtesy of S. Aikers

Having a RHIOT

Wildlife can be unpredictable in the best situations. When you are in the wilderness surrounded by forest you find yourself in their territory, and in their domain, anything can happen.

In 2007, Blaine and I both got accepted to do our RHIOT course up in Bamfield, B.C. and I was so ecstatic. I knew how hard it was to get into the course and how much fun it was going to be. There were two spots open, which worked out perfectly for both of us to go.

The course is provided by the Canadian Coast Guard and offered to other government agencies that work in the marine industry to help provide the necessary boat handling training out on the water. The course is always in the fall/winter up in Bamfield, B.C. on the west coast of Vancouver Island home to some of the harshest weather and sea conditions.

We were put up in a little Fishing Lodge for the week while we were training. It was the month of November and was especially snotty on the west coast of Vancouver Island that time of year.

We drove from Victoria all the way up to Bamfield (approximately 5hrs.) and it was a quiet drive up for the most part. Blaine and I sat in the backseat of the bus and we ended up picking up people in Nanaimo. We started talking to the other people who were going to be taking the course with us and found out that two of the participants were

RCMP officers needing boat training, and the other two were Coast Guard Employees from Sea Island Vancouver, and then of course Blaine and myself. I was the only girl of course, as per usual. You could say I was somewhat used to it by then.

On the way to Bamfield, we drove through Port Alberni, which had the last of the paved roads and then travelled on a gravel road for about an hour or so the rest of the way. About half way on the gravel road I had to pee very badly (stupid bumpy gravel road). It was extremely hard for me to hold it. Everyone knew I had to go badly and they were all trying to get me to go in the bush on the side of the road. There was no way that I was going to go off into the bushes and perhaps be eaten by a bear, a cougar, or worse.

We were almost at Bamfield but by that time I was jumping up and down in my seat because I had to go so badly. Finally, one of the RCMP officers said to me,

"Look just go already. We'll pull over and you can go in the bushes."

I snapped back at him, "Yeah sure I'll go in the bushes, but you'll be sorry when I get eaten by a bear."

It couldn't have been planned any better, at that precise moment, the bus had to slow right down to a stop because a black bear ran out and stopped in front of us.

I cried, "See, look a bear! I'm not crazy and I'm certainly not going to pee in the bushes."

I made him eat his words right then and there in front of everyone as they all started howling with laughter. I suffered in pain the rest of the way to the Lodge, but at least it was a good icebreaker and got everyone talking to one another. I finally got to go pee as soon as we arrived in Bamfield. We had to take a boat over to the Lodge where we were going to be staying for the week. The Lodge was cute and cozy and had a winter Lodge feel with a dark ambiance, a wood fireplace located in the middle of the main common room, and the rooms reminded me of being in a mountain chalet. They received a lot of business from people taking the course in the winter time, and in the summer, they always had a lot of tourists taking fishing charters and tours on the west coast.

The RHIOT course is only offered in the winter because the whole purpose of the course is to train you in the roughest conditions. The reasoning behind this is that usually when you get a SAR call it's not usually on a nice sunny day on flat calm seas. No, it's usually in snotty weather in rough sea conditions. *"A calm sea never made for a skillful sailor!"* (Roosevelt, D.F.1882-1945)

We were going to be learning how to handle the RHIBs in this type of weather because on the west coast of Vancouver Island you were never disappointed. Most often than not you would get rollers that were 30 ft. in height on an average day in the wintertime.

We were really going to have to listen to instructions because if you didn't, you could get yourself into trouble and fast. I'm not going to lie. I was scared shitless most of the time, but at the same time excited to have the power of the RHIB between my legs so I could push the limits of the boat as well as my own. I was eager to see what I could get out of the course, all the while feeling the fresh west coast air with the wind blowing ferociously against my face, leaving it raw and stinging. I was loving it!

The course was a lot of fun, and a lot of hard work. I got a sore back from being in the RHIB so long but nothing a soak in the hot tub couldn't fix back at the Lodge.

I was just so glad to have finished the course and to have passed. It was an intense course and overall a wonderful experience. I learned a lot about boats, about driving, and maintaining them. I also learned a lot about myself and about pushing boundaries.

I can honestly say it was probably one of the most memorable times of my life. What I would give to feel the throttle's blast of raw energy again, the rush of having the power of the engines at my fingertips.

We all packed up and headed on that bumpy gravel road back to Nanaimo to drop off one of the instructors, then back to Victoria where Blaine, the other instructor and I got off at the base.

I gave Blaine a ride home, then headed home myself. I was exhausted and sore from one hell of a week. No bears this time.

On my last day of RHIOT we took a picture of everyone dressed in his/her dry suits. Blaine, is 3rd from the right and Brianna is at the end on the right-hand side

-Photo courtesy of B. Snider

Think Pink

Written by Alena Mondelli

I am a sailor in the Royal Canadian Navy (RCN) and pink was never my favorite color.

However, in 2008, when I was promoted to Petty Officer 1st Class (PO1), I was the first Regular Force woman in my trade to do so. To mark the occasion, and with the encouragement from my husband, I bought myself a powder pink notebook cover: vinyl with a snap closure that comes up from the center right side. And it's that baby "breast cancer awareness" powder pink that does not, in any way, complement the dark blue of the Naval Combat Dress uniform.

I did wonder, for about five minutes, if maybe I was breaking a rule. The Canadian Armed Forces (CAF) has so many rules and regulations concerning the wearing of a uniform and what you can and can't wear with it. For example, I can carry an umbrella in uniform if it is black and in my left hand. This leaves the right hand free for saluting. I didn't see anything concerning non-conservative in color notebook covers. Besides, I would see the odd red notebook amongst a sea of black, gray, and dark green books. I felt justified with powder pink.

At the time of my purchase, I was the Senior Naval Communicator (Snr Nav. Comm.) onboard HMCS Vancouver and she was coming out of a 2-year refit period. My notebook

Women at Sea

went everywhere I went. It had to. I lived by lists, Post-it notes on random pages, and just having things written down all the time. It was a busy time with meetings all over the dockyard and the base. And, as you can imagine, everywhere I went someone in a very sarcastic voice would make the comment, "nice book." After a while the novelty of my book wore off and I had "forgotten" that it was pink. It was just my notebook, no color of note, and a vital tool in my day-to-day business toolbox.

After the ship Vancouver, I was posted for a year in Ottawa at National Defense Head Quarters (NDHQ) assisting in the frequency management of the Navy. I worked in an Industry Canada building that was gray-cubical central. Ottawa is a very political and conservative city. Everything has a place and an order to it. Surprisingly enough, my pink notebook was not even given a second glance. Now somewhere during this time I had also acquired a powder pink metal water bottle. I believe I had bought it, again with encouragement from my husband, on one of my vacation breaks back to Victoria. Now when I went to meetings, it was with my pink notebook and water bottle in hand. Occasionally, I would get an odd look from some long-in-the-tooth male Army member, but no one ever said anything.

After a year in Ottawa, I moved back to Victoria to spend a year learning how to speak French. It was obvious after spending a year in Ottawa, my French language skills were somewhat lacking. My pink notebook was replaced by a multitude of multi-colored binders and textbooks. My pink water bottle, on the other hand, became a training aid for learning French, and for that year was known as: ma bouteille d'eau rose.

Up until this point things have been quite uneventful. You are probably thinking, "What's the big deal about a powder pink notebook and water bottle?" And you're right; it's not a big deal. Sometimes I would randomly acquire the odd Bic Breast Cancer Awareness pen and I would be sporting all three!

71

Then I was posted to my current ship, HMCS Algonquin, where I am employed as the Combat Chief (CBTCH). It is a position for a Chief Petty Officer 2nd Class (CPO2) in one of the naval combat trades. I am no longer a tradesperson, but a manager and administrator of the Combat Department. In conjunction with my role as CBTCH, I am responsible for managing and planning the naval specific training of personnel onboard the ship (Training Chief), and the security of the ship (Force Protection Chief). Perfect for someone with powder pink things! A very good friend of mine had to celebrate the occasion by buying me a sparkly pink Swarovski crystal pen. Let me tell you, that puppy glistened and sparkled under the fake fluorescent lighting we have onboard the ship.

I was not the first but the second female CBTCH, and I believe the east coast has yet to have a female CBTCH. Female naval chiefs in the Regular Force in general are very, very rare. To some folks, a female supervisor is a big deal. Maybe even a novelty. There are positive and negative growing pains, trials, and tribulations for everyone. That's a story for another time. I digress...women have been sailing on RCN ships since 1989. When I joined Algonquin in July 2013, there were three senior female Non-Commissioned Members (NCM) of the rank of PO1 (one of them was a Warrant Officer, the Army equivalent to PO1). It was great to see. Two of them saw my powder pink notebook and went out and bought their own. The day the three of us showed up at a meeting all sporting pink books was priceless for me. Nothing like a) seeing senior ranking females in traditionally male-dominated positions, and b) seeing us doing that in pink! A very subtle way of saying, "I am a woman and I am proud!"

Last October I took some leave. Algonquin's sailing schedule was (and is) very extensive so sailors take leave when they can. When I came back and went into my office I noticed that someone had placed several boxes of pink-cased pens on my desk. I also noticed that I had a bunch of pink highlighters in my now pink (previously clear) pen holder. Right beside that was a pad of Hello Kitty Post-it notes. My personnel never really mentioned my pink notebook, pen or water bottle. But they acknowledged them in other ways, and they were very proud of themselves. So, I went with it. I always giggle when I send a file up to Command with a Hello Kitty Post-it note attached to it. Or, when I hand someone a pink pen and they ask me, "Is it blue ink?" Priceless. And last month they went one step further and painted the shelves in my office pink. Another "back off leave" surprise.

This leads me to my latest purchase: a stainless steel and pink travel tea/coffee press. Algonquin is heading out to sea for four months on deployment and this sailor needs to have a good cup of brewed caffeine. It will go nicely with my shelves as they are more of a deep pink than a powder pink. As a matter of fact, it will accent everything very nicely.

I'm sure my use of pink can be looked at very differently by different disciplines. But let's not analyze it too much. Let's just go with the thought that, "I might just like pink."

Alena in her uniform-Photo courtesy of A. Mondelli

A Shitty Situation

When you are a helmsman, there are certain times you cannot for any reason leave the ship's helm when you are steering in hand. This means that you control the ship with the ship's wheel and not the autopilot. For example, when you are in a tight narrow passageway or if you are in the middle of a big turn, you cannot do a handover midway because it could jeopardize the ship's steering. The relief doesn't know how the ship is handling as every ship handles differently in different weather, different tides, etc. To hand over the helm when you only have 100 ft. of water on either side of you is downright dangerous. The person on the helm already knows how the ship is handling and can maneuver to avoid tight situations accordingly.

The auto pilot can be unreliable at the best of times and you should still watch the helm closely even if the ship is in autopilot.

Of course, everyone must use the head at some point or another and on occasion you might have to go while you are steering the ship. You could do a handover with someone if you were in open waters and it wasn't so crucial that you stay on the helm. You could do the handover, run to the head, and come back. Unfortunately, there are times where you just can't do that handover (or if your watch partner is doing the hourly rounds and you have no one to relieve you) and, there are sometimes emergency situations you just can't avoid. The unavoidable happened to me while I was steering in hand on the helm of the ship. We were in a tight passage up in Llama Pass just south of Bella Bella, B.C. I was having stomach issues due to seasickness and eating leftovers from dinner the night before.

I had to do a bowel movement in a beastly manor. I just couldn't hold it any longer or I was going to burst. It wasn't protocol, to leave the wheel without doing a proper handover first. A proper handover consists of you telling the next person how the ship is handling, then you must say what course you are steering and then the person taking over must acknowledge it and repeat the course heading to make sure they heard you correctly. There was no time for that, none in the least. I grabbed my watch partner to take over as he had just come back from doing the hourly rounds and ran to the head as fast as I could, which was luckily located right beside the bridge on the ship I was on at the time.

Unfortunately for me, it was too late. I had already shit my pants and I had no time to deal with it. I had to get back on the bridge so that my watch partner could become look out again and I could become helmsman as we were navigating a tight pass with 100m on either side of the ship. We also didn't get to do a proper handover. I didn't know what to do. No time for clean-up, no time for anything. I had my heavy work boots on over my pants, so it would have taken me forever to take my boots off, pants off, and then my underwear. I thought to myself "what would MacGyver do?" I improvised and quickly grabbed my knife from my belt and cut my underwear on both sides so that I could easily take them off. (Every good sailor carries a knife on their belt). I cleaned myself up and threw the disposed pair of underwear in the garbage can and ran back to the bridge, commando, as fast as I could.

That experience will be permanently embedded in my brain as one of the most embarrassing, red-faced situations of my entire life. Remind me never to eat heated leftover dinner when I'm feeling sick. Not a great scenario, not a great ending. This is what I will be telling my grandkids one day.

These are the stories that get forever passed on from generation to generation.

When someone is feeling seasick and must be on the helm, someone usually just grabs a garbage can and puts it beside the helm in case of emergency. I don't know how many times I had to use this method (several) but it usually consisted of me steering then puking, then steering again, and then puking again when the ship was in any kind of rough weather. It was no fun. I quickly realized that I was not going to be going to sea for my entire career. I just couldn't put up with this for years to come, especially when we got into the especially rough weather in the winter time, and stuff is flying across the deck everywhere if not properly secured.

I learned an important lesson that day from my unfortunate mishap, always keep an extra pair of underwear in your pocket when you are up on the bridge just in case.

In Between a Boat and a Hard Place

Story by Stephanie Hamilton

Sometimes life throws us overboard and we need to pick ourselves back up, grab the life ring tossed our way, and carry on. The sea can be a dangerous place and in one precious moment, your life can change.

I didn't really know what I wanted to do in life. I didn't really imagine where I would end up or what I would be doing for my career. I had been a waitress/bartender almost my entire working career and wanted a change. If you told me what I would be doing at my age, I would never have believed you. I loved to SCUBA dive recreationally, so I went back to school and received my commercial diving license, from Seneca College. I could not find steady work in this field so a friend of mine told me I should consider becoming a diver for the Royal Canadian Navy.

I considered what qualifications I needed and what it meant to work for the Navy. I decided to join the Naval Reserves just to try it out first. You can leave anytime with notice and without signing a contract as you do with the Regular Force Navy. I found out I couldn't just become a diver with the Navy. I needed to do something else and work my way up to it, so I choose to become a Boatswain and eventually work as a Ship's team diver.

I did my basic training and then went to Halifax for three months to train and become a boatswain, learning everything from nautical terminology to training with the inflatable boats.

When my course was complete I was a bit anxious to go to sea. I received a contract in Victoria, B.C. and met my ship. I sailed one and two-month patrols at sea and soon found out that one of my more important jobs was to steer the ship at the helm or to be look out on the bridge. I was apprehensive at first that I was going to crash the ship because it was something so new to me. I didn't believe my crew when they told me what some of my duties were going to be.

It was an unusually snotty day out on the water and we were practicing for a Naval Boarding Party exercise departing our ship going to board another ship. I climbed over the side of the ship and was trying to make my way down the ladder to jump off the ship and onto the inflatable boat. I had my superior trying to tell me when to jump, as I had to time my jump properly with each wave that passed.

As I tried to jump from the ship to the inflatable the RHIB was coming up on top of a wave. As I stepped down, the RHIB took a dive and I suddenly fell into the warm waters of Puerto Vallarta between the ship and the RHIB. I have never been so scared in my life. My life jacket didn't inflate right away and with the weight of my clothes, my firearm, my heavy work boots and everything else, I submerged under the water and below the two boats.

One of my crew members had hold of me but let go when another crew member started to shout.

"Let go of her, let go of her!" he cried.

I finally popped back up behind the inflatable and my life jacket had finally inflated. My crew did a man overboard recovery and brought me back up into the inflatable, handed me a new life jacket, and carried on with the task at hand.

Women at Sea

When I think about it now and look back I think it's funny, but at the time I was scared for my life and I will never forget that experience. It was the inclement weather, and it was no one's fault, but I learned a lot that day. The sea is a dangerous place and that is why the Navy instills such good safety practices and procedures. They are there for a reason. I was just happy we were off the coast of Puerto Vallarta where the water was much warmer instead of the icy cold waters of the Pacific Northwest where hypothermia could have potentially set in quickly. I injured my shoulder during the whole ordeal and can never become a diver for the Navy because of it. I still dive on occasion for myself for recreation but because you must be in tip top shape to be a Ship's team diver I would unfortunately never meet the physical requirements.

During my time in the Navy, I have worked on several Maritime Coastal Defense Vessels (MCDV) and one Frigate. MCDV's patrol the coastal waters looking for illegal activity. A frigate is a high-speed large heavily armed sized war vessel. I have a shore position now, but I will go back to sea again in a couple of years. If I had it my way I would stay going to sea. I love it; I love every aspect of it especially travelling to all the different ports. I love exploring all the new places and seeing new sights. After my ordeal, we docked into Puerto Vallarta and a few crew members and I, on our days off, stayed at an all-inclusive resort for five nights while we were there, not many people can say they can do that with their job.

In my career, I have sailed on a ship with mostly female boatswains on board. We almost had an entire deck crew of women except for the Chief Boatswain's mate who was a man. That doesn't happen every day, especially when only about 19% of the Navy are women. I didn't mind it too much although some of the women especially the more petite ones had a hard time doing the same work as everyone else.

For me, I hope to have many more sea stories for years to come; life at sea isn't over for me just yet.

Thar, She Blows!

The sea is a magical place, full of life, plenty of fish, and mammals to see. Working on the water has its privileges as you get to enjoy and experience many different types of marine life.

Whether it be a seagull, a starfish, a whale, or even a fish, there is so much that the vast ocean can offer you. Some of us here on the west coast can often take the sea for granted being able to see it anytime we want to.

There are people all over the world who would pay big money to go on a guided fishing trip to catch a salmon for the first time, or go on a whale watching adventure to get a glimpse of an orca, or even bear watching along the coast in a guided helicopter just because it is a luxury for them and they may not live near the ocean.

I have been so fortunate to see what I have seen at sea. When I was living on our boat coming home at night, I saw more than a hundred-iridescent squid on the side of the dock all swimming in the same direction as a synchronized swimming team in the Olympics. It looked like they were glowing white in the nights shimmering blue waters.

We always had ducks and swans coming by our boat wanting to be fed. We would often give them breadcrumbs to eat to keep them coming back. They were gorgeous creatures. One year one of the swans came back by himself without his mate. I guess his mate must have died as swans always mate for life. It was sad watching him come back again and again roaming the water all by himself.

People who lived on their boats (liveaboards) would often get sea otters coming onto their decks and pooping all over their decks and the dock their boat was tied up to. An otter never dared come near our boat as we had a dog that neared a hundred pounds on our boat and could easily defend himself. Sea otters can be mischievous and can often be seen floating on their backs cracking open their dinner on their belly. They are cute when they are not pooping on your aft deck.

As I came home from work late one night, I spotted what I thought to be a cat at the end of one of the fingers on the dock. I thought it was one of the neighborhood cats that dropped in to say hello regularly, so I started to call it.

"Here kitty, kitty, kitty," I said.

I suddenly realized that it wasn't a cat, it was a raccoon and it was running straight for me because it felt trapped and cornered at the end of the finger. I just stood there helpless and tried to process everything that was happening when suddenly, it leapt towards me from the finger to the dock, missed the dock, and fell right into the water below. It swam under the dock, started to growl below my feet, then swam safely to shore. I'd never heard a raccoon growl before. It was not a happy camper.

My sister and I would often go shrimping or crabbing right off the dock by our boat. You must shrimp at night because that's when they come out of hiding and feed. All you need is a flashlight, a butterfly net and a bucket and you can catch them. They are very slow and easy to catch. Once we had caught enough, straight into the pot of boiling water they went, and you could shell them and eat them right away. We would set up a crab trap right over the side of the boat with some raw meat or a fish head in it for bait. We caught a few here and there and would eat them as an appetizer for dinner. We never really caught enough to have a crab feast.

If you looked under the dock you could often see starfish, barnacles, and sea anemones. Barnacles are so neat to see under the water when they are opened and feeding. Starfish are nature's very own color palette. With pretty colors like bright purples, oranges, and reds, they make the ocean colorful and beautiful to look at. Sea anemones are vibrant and beautiful too as they come in all different colors, shapes, and sizes. They are neat because of all their tentacles swaying under the water with the currents, it almost looks like a kite tail swaying back and forth in the wind only under the water.

Anytime you looked out onto the water you could be certain to see a shiny black head that belonged to a seal. They were usually bobbing their heads and fishing for fish or just plain curious about all the boats in the water. Sometimes, you would even get a fin slap on the water on occasion if one was trying to get your attention for some reason. On a rare occasion, you would even see a mighty sea lion propped up on the rocks or on top of a buoy warming themselves in the sunshine.

Often, if you looked up high in the sky you could see one or two eagles soaring above searching for their next meal. An eagle once came and swooped down to grab a seagull and tried to drown it. I think the seagull played dead because it lay limp in the water. When the eagle finally left it alone, the seagull got back up and flew away-a close call for sure. I've also seen several eagles swoop down and grab big salmon in their fierce talons. It's one of the coolest things to see on the water. Nature at its finest.

My friend and I were walking back to the dock one morning when we saw a seagull limping on the ground. It had a broken wing and couldn't fly so we ended up calling animal wildlife rescue. We were happy to do our good deed for the day, but I never found out of they could rehabilitate it.

They may have had to put it down depending on how severe the injury was. It must have been attacked by something to have been that injured.

When sailing at speed on the big ship we would often have visitors play in the bow and stern wake of the ship. As many as 50 Pacific white-sided dolphins would be playing, jumping, and gliding high above the waves crisscrossing back down storming the seas like lightning bolts. These dolphins are a little smaller and shorter than the bottlenose dolphin, but they are still magnificent creatures. When this happened, I would always say to myself, "I love my job".

One of my all-time favorite memories of wildlife at sea, was when I was on the deck of my ship as we were doing a safety/fire drill at anchor. I was waiting patiently at my muster station waiting for the signal to return to my cabin when suddenly, three or four humpback whales started breaching out of the water nearby. They started jumping wholeheartedly out of the water doing belly flops, jumping, and playing. I was so envious of their freedom to move about like they did in the open ocean. It was a spectacular show they were putting on for us and I had a front row seat on a beautiful sunny day. Several other encounters with whales left me breathless, one being I saw a pod of orcas (or killer whales as they are commonly known as) swim past our ship far off in the distance. I knew they were killer whales by their black and white dorsal fin. These majestic creatures roam and play in earth's oceans as their playground. When I come back, I want to be a whale.

The sea is truly a magical place. Mother Nature's best kept secret.

Brianna Snider

Sea Lion in Patricia Bay, Victoria, B.C.

-Photo courtesy of B. Snider

The Great White North

Story by Jackie Grant

While on a ship, being diligent with safety and the safety of the crew is always preferable. Unfortunately, accidents do happen and when they do, it is often in a remote location with limited access to a hospital or clinic.

Ever since I was little my parents always had a boat. My dad was a fisherman on the St. Lawrence River, and I used to go with my grandpa down on the docks to see the big ships dock. I was always on or around the water and I always knew I wanted to work on a ship.

As a Navigation Officer, I started my training in 2001 doing the Watch keeping Mate program. I attended three years of school and worked one year at sea as a cadet. I trained on different types of ships such as tankers, scientific research vessels, container ships, bulk carriers, self-unloaders, and general cargo ships with cranes. I took courses such as basic knot tying, astronavigation, ship's stability, and collision regulations.

During my time as a cadet, I worked two weeks down in the engine room to learn a bit about the inner workings of a ship's engine room. If I hadn't been accepted into school to become a navigator, I would have become an engineer. I am quite glad I became a Navigation Officer after all as I don't think I could stand the smell of the engine room for very long. They also never see the light of day as they are stuck down at the bottom of the ship for long periods, usually without a porthole to look out from.

Working away had its disadvantages. Some of the companies I worked for were short staffed, so they would ask me to stay longer until they could find relief. A normal work day consists of six-hours on six-hours off. It was really tiring towards the end of a patrol and I would quickly burn out.

As a ships officer, I would have my meals made for me every day from the fabulous cooks onboard. I also loved not having to clean while onboard the ship (my cabin is cleaned, and my bunk is always made for me.)

Some captains didn't like having a female onboard and some would talk down to me or talk about me or about women in general in front of me to other men. In a sense, it was a form of harassment because I felt belittled, like I needed to fight for my place on the ship on a constant basis. These are only some of the challenges that came with being a woman sailor.

I also had men that tried to woo me with candy and wine. One deckhand left a bag of candy on my bunk in my cabin and I was freaked out that he had been in my cabin. He said it was because he was thanking me for being his friend, but I felt there was more to it. Another crew mate gave me a bottle of wine for my birthday and asked me to bring it down to his cabin and drink it. I didn't feel comfortable doing so, so I gave the bottle of wine away and said no thank you.

I finished a patrol with one company when my boyfriend Nate and I got a job offer on another vessel up north. It was an opportunity to try something different, as we personally knew the Captain and he wanted me to work as a Helmsman for the trip instead of my regular job as a mate. I had worked three years as a mate up north and three years as a first mate on the great lakes with plenty of navigation experience. Now was my chance to do something different. I sailed my first and only patrol as a helmsman, just off the shores of

Baffin Island in Pond Inlet when I was trying to climb up the ladder of a container on a container ship. Winter conditions made for a cold and icy trip. Slushy snow lay at the foot of the ladder where my foot touched the ladder and suddenly, I found myself flying backwards onto the deck below, feet still attached to the ladder and all I could see was the gloomy sky up above.

Luckily, I was wearing heavy clothing and lots of layers, which must have saved me from really hurting my back when I struck the hard steel deck. My ankles, however, were badly hurt and I couldn't walk. Several crew members assisted me to my feet and helped carry me out and up several flights of stairs. It isn't easy getting around on a rolling ship without the use of your legs.

My feet were so swollen I first thought they were both broken. The crew then put me into a smaller boat and took me ashore to get them looked at, loaded me up on wooden pallets and forklifted me to the only clinic in town to take x-rays, as there were no cars in sight. When we arrived at the clinic, there was one nurse there who was a local Inuktitut woman. She spoke to me in broken English as she examined me.

She looked at my ankles, took one look at my bruised-up legs (from working on deck) and thought that my crew members were beating and abusing me. I kept trying to convince her that I was fine and that the crew members on the ship were nice and that my boyfriend was onboard to "protect me".

I stayed onboard the ship and did minimum duties. My ankles weren't broken but badly bruised; I knew they would heal with time. I really didn't want to leave the ship, as it was my only shot at working as a deckhand instead of a mate and Nate was also onboard and I didn't want to leave him. We were even able to share a cabin that patrol. Why would I want to leave?

Although we shared a cabin, Nate and I were on opposite watches so while he was working I would be sleeping and vice versa. The only contact we had with each other was cleaning the mess that the other person left behind in the cabin. It's like we were two strangers passing each other as shadows in the night.

Now, I am still going to sea working as a mate for the B.C. Ferries. Nate and I would like to settle down and start a family soon. I am still very career-oriented and driven and I will be writing my Master Mariner's certificate soon. It has always been my dream to become a Captain of my own ship and now my dream will finally become a reality. I don't know if I will always go to sea. If I have kids it might change things, but at least I have my certifications and have options for shore positions. My goal is to become a Compass Adjuster one day and do a magnetic swing on some of the larger ships.

My story is far from over. There are more sailing adventures waiting for me to have alongside Nate, my partner in crime. From working during my patrol as a deckhand, I learned to always be aware of your surroundings and the importance of ship safety. Ship safety being especially important when on a rolling ship on the outside deck and surrounded by the elements. Anything can happen when you are at sea, so always be prepared.

Women at Sea

Jackie cruising the East Coast of Canada
-Photo courtesy of J. Grant

Jackie working on deck as a deckhand
-Photo courtesy of J. Grant

⚓

Anchors Aweigh in Mozambique

Written by Jen Scott

When life gives you challenges, you must overcome adversity, stay strong, and turn to your fellow man for assistance putting all pride aside.

I have lived and worked on the water all my life. My parents bought their first 36' troller, the Wandelaine, in 1971 and still own her today. We adventured and fished up and down the coast until the collapse of the Southern Gulf fishery in the late 1990's. The memories of my childhood are strongly ingrained with the people and communities that made up the commercial fishery on our coast. Sadly, most of this is gone now, but if you go down to a dock and happen to meet a fisherman like my Dad working on his old boat he may invite you into the cabin, warm and cozy with the oil stove burning and hear some of the best stories of how life used to be on this coast and the people we called friends and family. It is these stories that have made me who I am. And I am proud to be a boat kid born and raised.

I was about 20 years old when the fishing industry started to fall apart. Over fishing, poor stock management, and the rise in water temperature, had finally started to pay its price. We followed the fish and travelled up to the north coast and fished for spring salmon off Haida Gwaii for a couple of years. My son was a year old at the time. We built a play pen for him down in the fo'c'sl and he loved being on the boat. I would be in the back running the gear, my Dad the Captain trying to find some fish and my Mom cooking pancakes for breakfast.

My son is another coastal kid in the making. I went into labor at nine and a half months pregnant on the back of the boat during a sockeye opening in Johnstone Strait in August of 2006. I had to cut a hole in my rain gear to fit my big belly and had spent 18-hours in the back of the boat the day my son decided to arrive. I am pretty sure I still smelt like sockeye slime in the hospital when he was born.

But back in the 1990's when fishing slowed, and I had time, I went travelling. In 1995, I went to Africa and I went back again in 2000 and lived and worked in Mozambique. Mozambique is a beautiful country on the east coast of Africa that was ravaged by civil war from 1977-1992. When I was there in 1995 the country had just opened to foreigners, there was no electricity, and very little infrastructure. Most of the country was riddled with landmines and whole areas were no go zones where the mines had yet to be cleared. When I returned in 2000 much had changed and although it was still an extremely poor country, it had started to attract visitors from South Africa and Europe. In a town called Vilankulos, a 38' Catamaran was anchored out in the bay for a couple of months. Turns out they were looking for a crew to do dive and fly-fishing tours and the Captain asked me to join. So, two local guys who spoke only Portuguese, myself, and our never sober South African Captain, made up the crew of the little catamaran.

As the only woman on board, who happened to be white, speak little to no Portuguese and had no sailing but lots of ocean experience, it was up to me to befriend and somehow win over the two local men who had absolutely no idea what to make of me. But in very little time Castigo, Lukas, and I, became great friends and they taught me how to rig a sailboat, navigate the ever-changing sand bars, and speak passable but often hilarious Portuguese. These men had grown up on this stretch of coast and knew it intimately. And although at first, they did not know what to make of a skinny white girl giving them orders, I think my deep respect for their knowledge and my willingness to ask for their guidance helped us form a great friendship. My main concern was dogging the sand bars and keeping the German tourists from drowning. And as all the local sailors used a form of celestial navigation, no charts or navigational equipment, I relied on Castigo and Lukas, and their local knowledge to keep us safe.

After a year of living and working in Mozambique, with many great new boat stories to tell, I returned home to B.C. and went back fishing for a while then started a family. We lived on Hornby Island, where my parents had settled, and we were flat broke, as most young families are, and I needed something more stable financially than fishing. So, I swallowed my pride and applied to B.C. Ferries. Turns out they weren't hiring on Hornby, so I ended up calling the Canadian Coast Guard. The HR woman I spoke to told me to get my MED's and challenge my Bridge watchman ticket, which I promptly did. I was hired two weeks later as a deckhand to sail up to the Arctic on a light icebreaker, the *CCGS Sir Wilfrid Laurier*.

I remember my first day on the Laurier. She was tied up alongside at the Victoria CCG base loading for a buoy trip. I showed up at the office and signed my contract of employment, picked up the dreaded uniform and walked down the long jetty towards this massive red steel ship with a helicopter sitting on the aft deck. I had worked on boats all my life but never on a ship. *The Laurier* was the largest ship in the Coast Guard's Pacific fleet. She looked massive and I remember thinking that it was time to seriously pull up my big girl panties and just put one foot in front of the other. I came to love that ship and my time on her was some of the most memorable of my time at sea. Part of this was the experience of getting to see so much of the Pacific coast but also venture up in to the western and central arctic. The first time I went up to the Arctic on *The Laurier* I remember following the Great Circle Route and as we passed the northern tip of Haida Gwaii thinking this is it; this was new territory on our coast that I had never been to. It was a different kind of ocean, a different kind of swell, color, and wind pattern, I was enthralled. Everything about the Arctic, once we made the two-week trip and rounded Cape Barrow to start down the Northern Slope, is alien and new. The air is different, being so crisp and clean and the water changes from different shades of aquamarine to deep ocean blue. The 24-hours of daylight takes a bit of getting used to. But sitting on the aft deck having a beverage in the bright sun at 2:00am after a long 12-hour shift is spectacular. And later in the season when the sun starts to set again, the northern lights come out to play and turn the sky in to a dancing, pulsing, dreamscape, that truly needs to be seen to be believed.

Working on *The Laurier* was not all fun and adventure. It was extremely hard physical labor and the daily demands taught me how to be a sailor through blood, sweat, and tears. It took a lot to prove that I was strong enough to work on that ship, broken fingers and dislocated ribs. It took a while to prove that I could pull my weight and deserved the respect of my fellow deckhands. But those boys and I had a hell of a good time and we became a family. Many of them still work in the marine industry and I proudly call them my brothers to this day.

One of the most fun parts of working up in the Arctic is the ice. Navigating through ice goes against everything I had learned throughout my life. Ice, is this big white icy landscape that is displayed in front of you like a massive island and my first instinct was to avoid hitting it all costs. But when sailing on an icebreaker, you find a track to follow, take a good run at it, and hit it as hard as you can. And I mean ramming the ice hard. The idea is that the ship doesn't so much ram the ice and break it, it rides up onto the ice and the weight of the vessel crushes the ice below. You then back up carefully as to not get ice chunks in the propellers, pick up ramming speed, hit the ice, and ride up again as far as you can go. The ship shudders, shakes, and leans surprisingly far over as it smashes and cracks the ice underneath it. Reverse and repeat. The ship will continue like this following a "lead" or clear path to get to where we needed to go. Often when navigating in the Arctic, it is more slowly picking your way through chunks of older ice that is already broken. When it was time to break ice, everything on board would be tied down and the cooks and galley crew would be cursing and swearing as their dishes shuddered and smashed upon impact. No one got any sleep while breaking ice.

I worked for the Coast Guard for almost three years and then it was time to come home to my son and not be away at sea anymore. My son needed me, and although it was hard to leave a job I loved, I knew that I loved my son much more. I did join B.C. Ferries and during my time working for them, I obtained my Watchkeeping Mate certificate. At the time of my resignation from B.C Ferries in 2017, I was working as the Chief Officer on the *Queen of Cumberland* out of Swartz Bay. I enjoyed my time with B.C. Ferries, mostly the people I worked with and friends I made. I left with a good feeling of having accomplished one step further in my marine career as a supervising officer and I'm grateful for that opportunity.

The life of a sailor is a hard one. You make a lot of sacrifices to love the sea. The respect it takes to co-exist with that kind of powerful force will make you a certain kind of person in this world. I think it has helped make me the woman I am today. And all the people I grew up fishing with, and worked with through my marine career, have helped create the stories that I tell. I am proud of these stories and my life at sea.

Women at Sea

Jen on a fishing boat catching a salmon

-Photo courtesy of J. Scott

Pregnant at Sea

Story by Paula White

When you are in the middle of the ocean away from hospitals and medical care, anything can happen. You pray that you aren't the one that requires medical attention minutes, if not hours, away from shore and stuck in the middle of the ocean.

I started with the B.C Ferries 18 years ago, when I was only 21 years old. I never imagined what an exciting career it had the potential to become. No one day is ever the same. It could be because the weather has changed, and we are in the middle of a wind storm, or that fact that we get famous people riding on our ships all the time. I once met Ben Kingsley Oscar winning actor and Dave Barrett, a former Premier of B.C. It is never boring, and no one-day is ever the same.

Everyone who works on the water is proud, especially those working for the B.C Ferries. If there is a Search and Rescue call on one of our routes, we are normally one of the first responders as we are most likely the closest to help those in trouble. It is our duty to help and join with the Coast Guard on certain calls and they rely on us to be there when they can't be. Anything from helping kayakers to over turned fishing boats.

As a Customer Service Attendant onboard a B.C Ferry boat I am kept very busy. On the boats I have done a variety of jobs such as cashier, galley helper, and first aid attendant. I also have been a longtime shop steward and local One president for B.C Ferry Marine Workers Union, a strong passion of mine.

It took me seven years to get a permanent job with the ferries, and during that time I worked casual-on-call and never knew when I was going to work next. They would literally call me half an hour before a shift started to ask if I'd come into work. I did not mind though, as this was back before I had my kids. For someone who has kids, it's not the best job to start out with. It would be hard to find daycare I would imagine. That would be when a live-in nanny might just come in handy.

I started school to become a nurse and ended up not liking it. I changed my schooling and transferred to school at the University of Victoria, during which time I applied for the B.C Ferries to make some money. I already had some sailing certificates and had previously been a first aid attendant, so it was natural for me to apply there as I have always loved the ocean. When I was younger I went on a family trip to England and found out my great-great grandfather had been a lifeboats man, as had his father and brother. So, in fact, I come from a long line of seafarers.

I have always been around the ocean. I have lived on Vancouver Island my entire life. The pristine wilderness and wildlife that surrounds us, and all the little islands in amongst the big island that makes up this beautiful landscape. We are so lucky to live here and every day I love sitting in my office which is just a table next to a window on the ferry. I never know if I am going to see whales, or dolphins, or a big cargo ship that has come half way around the world. Last summer I even saw a burning boat in Swartz Bay. Even though I clean toilets for a living, I can honestly say I love my job and I would not have it any other way. I do not think I could work in an office Monday to Friday working inside eight-hours a day. That's just not me.

I love taking pictures of all the beautiful sunsets and sunrises. When you start work at 5:00am in the morning and work late, sometimes until 10:30pm at night, you see some amazing sights. The reds, oranges, and pinks, in the sky create the most amazing landscape photographs. I am constantly taking pictures from the boat. How lucky I am to be surrounded by this breathtaking scenery and to be able to see wildlife anytime I want outside my window. For me, it's love. I love everything about it and every day, I am completely and utterly mesmerized by what I see outside my window.

When I worked as a first aid attended on some of the ships it was a challenge. I had to deal with things like women miscarrying on the ship, and other medical emergencies. You don't realize how isolated you are from everything if something ever did happen. You just hope that when you put out that call on board over the ships P.A for a nurse or a doctor to help, that someone comes to your assistance. Otherwise, it's all on you until the ferry docks on the other side for paramedics to come to your rescue.

Working on a ferry boat, you are also exposed to a lot of different illnesses, having a high turnover of people from all parts of the world on the ship at any given time. There are always at least a few people with colds or the flu, and of course they are touching surfaces on board that other people touch, and it spreads like a wildfire. If one person on a ship is sick, everyone gets sick. When a cruise ship has an outbreak of an illness or disease when they dock here in Victoria or Vancouver, they normally must ride the ferry home to wherever they are going and that's how the diseases spread.

The hardest part of my job would be when I was pregnant both times with my kids. Working in a mostly male dominated workplace was hard enough during the best of times. When your pregnant on board, sometimes it was hard for my coworkers to understand how I was feeling, or what I was going through.

The first time I was pregnant on the ship with my oldest daughter, I worked in the galley on the large boats. The major issues I ended up having was extreme morning sickness. I couldn't stand the smells coming from the galley. The smell of clam chowder in the morning was my undoing every day of my pregnancy. The boat moved, and I was sick. I ended up being off for a month. I tried many times coming back to work that month, but only made it as far as the parking lot before becoming ill again. Once the first few months of morning sickness had passed the pregnancy went well. I was lucky that on the boat I was working on I was able to work with one of my best friends. He made sure I was not lifting anything too heavy and had my back. On a large boat with a large crew the ratio to men and women is more even. More hands to help you. They were also more use to women being pregnant in the work place on a bigger vessel. I made it to two months before I was to have my daughter and went off on vacation until I had her.

Now my second pregnancy could not have been more different. Small crew with two women employees and the rest of the crew being men. This time I was working on a small boat. I was ok for the first six months of my pregnancy but was then switched to an even smaller boat with no elevator in my final trimester. I had to go up and down a lot of stairs all the way up from the car deck up to the snack bar. This was about three stories up. Some men would stand idly by while I was huffing and puffing up the stairs carrying heavy loads with my big belly in tow, while a select few would stop to help me. It felt like chivalrous men were a thing of the past. I never worked any less because I was pregnant, even though some crew members may say otherwise. I merely took it easier on some jobs because of my condition. I may not have vacuumed the ship as fast as I normally would have during my pregnancy, but I tried my best to live up to the standards put forth by those around me. It was a completely different experience. I think that most of the male crew members weren't necessarily used to working with a lot of females, especially pregnant ones.

This pregnancy however, would not go as smooth as the first one. To this day I curse that small boat with no elevator. The first one I was on was a large boat with a large first aid room. It had everything you needed to deliver a baby. The little boats did not. With the little boats, also came routes much farther from medical aid, and crew with much lower first aid training. I felt uneasy most of the pregnancy about being on a small boat that was also much slower than some of the larger boats. If I were to go into labor, who would help me and how long would it take to get me medical help? Being on a much more physically demanding boat, with more stairs, more lifting, and having to climb up and down on benches to do blinds, made it much more challenging. At 34-weeks, I started to feel sick. I couldn't put my finger on it, but something was not right. That day I called in to work sick. I later heard from one of my co-workers that one of my male co-workers thought I was milking the pregnancy thing. I felt horrible and I couldn't believe he would say something like that. That night at about 1:00am I started to have cramping. I was so scared because it wasn't contractions like I had with my first pregnancy. It was one big long cramp. I had known a coworker that had a still born at this time and I was so scared I had pushed myself too hard at work. I got mad at my husband in the middle of the night for snoring and had sent him to the spare room. I lied there thinking about all the worst possible things that could be happening with my body and to my baby. Finally, at about 5:00am I woke my husband up. I was in tears because I was still cramping and had no water breaking or contractions. I was also only 34-weeks which is very early to be in labor. At 7:00am we called the doctor, he told me to hang tight. We waited until after lunch and nothing had let up. We then had to go to the hospital to see what was going on. Upon arrival, I found out I was in labor. That I was 5cm dilated and that I would be having the baby that day.

Of course, my first thoughts were, "What!? Are you going to stop this? I don't have a car seat. I have another two weeks of work. Something is wrong here!"

I called into work that night to tell them I was having the baby. I remember thinking to myself, "I can't wait for my co-workers to find out I had the baby. I hadn't been milking a thing!"

I am so thankful I called in sick that day. It saved mine and my youngest daughter's life. What would have happened if I was stuck on a boat in the middle of a ferry run with no nurse, and no doctor onboard? It would have taken a minimum of an hour to get back to land and then to the hospital. Thank goodness for woman's intuition. Minor cramping, very low blood pressure and 12-hours later, I gave birth to my second daughter who is now three years old.

I am now only working part-time as my youngest daughter is still little. I can job share with another person, so it works out perfectly for my schedule. Between my husband and I and both of us working shift work, we don't have to pay for daycare which is a bonus. The fact that I rarely get to see my husband is beside the point.

Maybe I will go back to work full-time once my kids are in school, but for now I will continue to work part-time and stay home as much as possible. I will most likely stay working with the B.C. Ferries until I retire. It's an excellent paying job and, because I have seniority, they accommodate the needs of my family. I would recommend working for the B.C Ferries for anyone wanting to pursue a career at sea. It is the only sailing job where you get to come home to your family every night!

B.C Ferry off the coast of beautiful Vancouver Island, B.C
-Photo courtesy of P. White

The bow of a B.C Ferry

-Photo courtesy of P. White

Descendants from the Bounty

Story by Heather Carlson

Everyone has a story to tell, some more believable than others. When sailing the globe, you just never know what or who you may come across.

As a First Officer onboard a private yacht that travels the world, I came across many things, but nothing could have prepared me for what I was about to witness just off the coast of Tahiti. I have worked on oil tankers, cruise ships, yachts, and I also spent some time working on shore working as a nautical manager and a yacht manager. I had always dreamed of going to sea when I was young and going on sailing trips with my dad in Northern Alberta. I never imagined it would lead me to such an elaborate lifestyle and seeing wonderful new ports around the world at each turn. When at sea, I would be contracted for four months on, two months off, but normally I stayed with the ship longer as it was often difficult to find relief to replace me.

I started out when I was 21 and did a four-year navigation program at BCIT Marine campus in North Vancouver. I ended up on an oil tanker as a cadet and learned the hard way that it wasn't normal for women to be a sailor on a big ship. There were a lot of men on the oil tanker that didn't believe women should be working at all, let alone working in a job that they were doing.

After working on the oil tanker, I graduated from BCIT, and then went on to work for a cruise line onboard a ship that travelled the world. I was so lucky in that respect because I wasn't stuck on a cruise ship that did the same leg repeatedly. I could see many exotic ports in parts of the world that are not travelled as much as others.

One of my favorite places I visited was in Southern Argentina in Ushuaia. It is the most southern port you can go to, so I'm proud to say I have been to the most southern tip of the world. When we were tied up there, the wind was blowing about 50 knots/hr. We threw on an extra hawser line that we called "The Beast" because it was so massive and would help keep the ship from bashing around on the dock. I was on the mooring deck working when suddenly, one of the spring lines broke and whizzed past my head in a fury. The line had hit the steel bulkhead and dented it about an inch. I could have easily died in that moment if it had hit me, but luckily it didn't even touch me. I will never forget that close call.

On my travels we also steered the ship 1000 miles up the Amazon River and ended up in the middle of the jungle in Manaus. Trying to steer on a river with six knots of current beneath the water's surface was difficult. We didn't want to get shipwrecked or run aground by any means with the looming threat of piranhas' and crocodiles in the river below us. Those were just some of the scary components of navigating up the Amazon.

Another place we sailed to was Christmas Island, a territory of Australia in the Indian Ocean. In the 1950s, the tiny island was subject to British Nuclear Weapons tests. This was another place we were told to never run aground, as the waters were shark infested and dangerous due to previous nuclear testing. Nothing like the threat of being eaten by a shark or being blown up to bits!

It was so interesting to see these places with my own eyes. It seemed surreal and I felt so lucky to witness all the many miracles of the world at sea. When we were on the Baltic Sea near Estonia in Poland, far off in the horizon I could see the Northern Lights overhead in the night sky. Not everyone gets to see such a magnificent sight in his or her lifetime. I also saw the sun setting on the horizon and the moon rising at the exact same time. It was magical.

As we were coming up to this tiny island in the middle of the South Pacific Ocean with no other land in sight for miles, I hailed someone over the VHF. We were talking with them for a while to figure out their story and to find out why people were living on this tiny landmass in the middle of nowhere. The story we heard was almost as unbelievable as the people living there.

In 1790, nine of the mutineers from a British Royal Navy ship called *"The Bounty"* inhabited Pitcairn Island along with several Tahitians' to form a small colony on the island. The ship was commandeered by one of the ship's crew members, which led to a mutiny against the Captain on April 28th, 1789. Approximately half of the crew were resistant, and the other half supported the mutiny. Some crew members fled to Tahiti where they were captured and put on trial. Some escaped to an uncharted island called Pitcairn Island and the descendants from the mutineers still live on the tiny island working and farming the lands to this day. The people don't generally leave the island unless they are sick or imprisoned, but they do have basic amenities such as a post office, public school, museum, and a few attractions for people visiting the island. To think these people, live hundreds of miles away from even the nearest Polynesian island was hard for me to wrap my head around. The islands inhabitants were less than 100 people and the pristine waters that surrounded the tiny island are home to many endangered species of fish and mammals.

The settlers that burned *The Bounty* in what is now called Bounty Bay on Pitcairn Island, did it so there would not be any evidence of the mutiny occurring and to hide from the British Navy as it was a great offence against the crown to form a mutiny. The settlers also went on to change their names and have families of their own. The people who live on the Island now are all descendants from the Mutiny on the Bounty that happened so long ago. In 1960, the American Navy made a replica of the Bounty which later floundered and sank in 2012 during Hurricane Sandy. One of the descendants from the original Mutiny of the Bounty was on it and perished at the time.

As much as I love the ocean and working on it, eventually my fiancé and I would like to start our own family. I do hope to acquire enough sea time to be able to write my Master Mariners certificate next year. My fiancé is from New Zealand, so we are planning on moving there and settling down after the wedding and hopefully starting a family. I love working at sea, but I am now ready and up for the challenge of becoming a mom. For those of you wanting to pursue a career at sea, don't do it just for the money; if you don't love it, you will be miserable and may end up starting your own mutiny at sea.

Heather working on deck of an oil tanker as a cadet

-Photo courtesy of H. Carlson

Old Traditions Die Hard

I was very lucky being on the ship that I was on for my first ship. The crew, especially the boatswain, were very traditional sailors. They believed very much in keeping the different sailing traditions alive.

One patrol, my crew change took place on Boxing Day, which meant we were all going to be spending New Year's on the ship. My shift was from midnight to noon, so I couldn't celebrate much beyond helping all the people enjoying themselves back to their bunks.

We were anchored in Port Alice and all day long the crew were razzing me because I was the youngest person onboard the ship, threatening to make me dress up as the New Year's Baby and wear nothing but a diaper. There was one other guy, Blaine (my now husband), who was a week younger. He got to wear a banner, but they still tried to get me to wear the stupid diaper.

They tried to coax me out of my cabin before I started my watch, but I knew what they were trying to do. I stayed in my cabin with the door locked right up until the very last minute before I had to go up to the bridge and do a watch change. I ran up the back stairs, so no one would see me. One of the other crew members ended up wearing the diaper just for fun. (Let's just say he was having a little too much fun). At midnight, because Blaine was wearing the New Year's banner, he got to ring the ship's bell. Six times to ring out the old year and six times to ring in the new one, a long-standing tradition on board the ship.

Other traditions on the ship consisted of hand waxing the sailmakers twine instead of using pre-waxed twine. The Boatswain would also ring the ship's bell every time a shot would come up on the anchor chain when heaving the anchor. One shot is equal to 15 fathoms converted to 90 ft. If four shots were out at anchor when the third shot came up, the Boatswain would ring the bell three times. When the second shot came up he would ring it two times, and when the last shot came up he would ring the bell once. This lets the bridge know how much anchor chain is still on the bottom. When the anchor breaks away from the bottom of the ocean, the Boatswain rings the bell continuously to let the bridge and the Captain know "anchor aweigh".

We also did a lot of canvas work onboard the ship during our slow times to make covers and bags all hand stitched. I think it was mostly to keep us busy when things were slow, but it is a great asset to have especially if you need to patch a sail. Every good sailor knows how to sew.

A ship faithfully keeps record of business that happens onboard in the ship's logbook. It is the quartermaster's job to update the weather by the hour (taken from the barometer) so that the Mates and Captain can see the weather pattern (see pg. 210). A change in pressure can tell you if a storm is coming. It's up to the Mates and Captain to update the ship's log of anyone coming onboard or leaving the ship as well as all-important activity. The logbook is an official document that can be used in court to provide an accurate recollection of what really happens onboard the ship should an incident occur.

A Jacob's ladder is traditionally handmade of rope and wood, and hangs over the side of the ship so that crew can get from the ship to shore or from the ship to another vessel. In rougher sea conditions, you must time it right so that you jump from the ladder to the other vessel on the top of a wave and don't get squished between the ship and the vessel. You don't want to "get stuck in between a rock and a hard place" as the saying goes.

Every true sailor knows how to do knot work. I was lucky because the ship I was on made all their own fenders and bumpers, also known as "sausages". These are designed to protect the ship from rubbing against other vessels or the dock. The cheap plastic ones you can buy at the store are offensive to traditional sailors and no one likes an old rope fender more than a true sailor.

Onboard my ship the Leading Seamen were the ones who made new rope and wire "snotters". A snotter is a line or wire with eyes spliced into both ends. It is mainly used for hooking up loads to the crane but has many other purposes.

I felt honored to learn these traditions from such experienced sailors. It was a pleasure to work with them, even though they razzed and harassed me so much of the time. They knew what they were talking about, having received their knowledge from generations of sailors before them. My Boatswain's father was a sea Captain, so he decided to take on the sailor life and follow in his father's footsteps. I will never forget the things I learned and the stuff he showed and taught me. I hope that one day I can pass down some of these traditions to my kids.

There was so much to learn, so much to know. I don't know how any person could remember to do everything. I guess with time and practice one could become a great sailor. For some, it takes years of service to master the skills of sailing. It helps when original traditions are passed down from the old salty sea dogs down to the greenhorns coming up the Hawse pipe.

Sailing Woes

Story by Karry Lowes

Those little moments when you realize your life hangs in the balance are the scariest you will ever have to face.

I was 200 miles offshore with my then boyfriend in a little 30ft. slew sailboat. Hitting 12ft. swells that were cresting over the entire boat amongst bad weather, I felt our lives were in jeopardy if I didn't take over command of the boat.

As a captain for hire, I do anything from cooking, to deckhand, to mate, to captain. I currently hold my U.S 100-ton Inland Captain's certificate. I have sailed on ships such as passenger ferries, sail training vessels (otherwise known as tall ships), tug boats, and chartered yachts in the British Virgin Islands.

I started sailing when I was 25 years old and worked on the Victoria Clippers for five years to acquire experience and sea time. My favorite part of going to sea has always been the boating community and watching the dynamics of the crews onboard the ships. It's so different from working a shore job working 9-5 days and heading home at the end of a work day. When you're at sea your shipmates become your family. They see you when you are at your best, but they also see you after your watch is over, in your pajamas, even without make-up.

I started working at sea to get into the travel business and see different parts of the world. I have always worked with other women sailors on all the ships I've been on except for tugboats. Tugboats are very dangerous and there are many old "Sea dogs" still working on them with their traditional ways of thinking. Working on the tugs I felt like a lot of the men didn't want me there and were wondering why I was even there in the first place.

The reason my offshore trip was such an important event in my life was because it allowed me to finally stop underestimating and doubting myself. I stopped deferring to a partner just because he owned the vessel and called himself the skipper. While preparing for that trip I had a job driving a passenger ferry that carried 250 passengers and two crew, all of whom were my responsibility in addition to the operation of the boat. Yet I found myself falling into a "pink" mentality of catering to my partner's ego and masculinity by letting him call all the shots, even though my life was technically on the line.

We were in 12' swells, about nine seconds apart, with 5ft. wind waves, cresting all around the small sailboat. I was alone at the helm, with my PFD harness on and clipped into ringbolts within the cockpit. I looked around and realized that at some point, a wave was going to crash right on top of the boat. He was resting below, all hatches closed. Within minutes a wave did finally crest right on my head and "pooped" the boat. But we were still flying along at nine knots, I sat there, soaked and up to my knees in water because the cockpit wasn't draining. It must have been 30 seconds before he even poked his head out of the cabin to see if I was ok. Now this wave had truly slammed on to the boat, and it would have sounded catastrophically loud below in the cabin. At first, I laughed, having predicted this and realizing there's nothing I could do about being all wet. Then I was wondering why he hadn't come up to check on me sooner. If I were to leave the tiller, the boat would founder, so I remained clipped in and kept steering.

When he finally popped his head up, I asked "How come you didn't check on me right away?"

He replied, "I was afraid you were washed overboard, and that another wave might wash me overboard too."

Then he saw the cockpit full of water and freaked out. I figured the water would drain eventually, but it was going a little too slow for my liking. The cockpit wasn't very big. He sounded desperate to find a solution and said he was going to disengage the cockpit drain hoses. These led from under the cockpit, into the cabin, and down and out through through-hulls at the bottom of the boat. I instantly saw his exhaustion, his desperation and the potential for a seacock to fail or another wave to crash onto the boat during this process, and of course none of it made sense because then where would the water drain to? Into the cabin? At that moment I became the leader, and I think he was relieved, because he was truly exhausted. I firmly said that we would not be detaching the cockpit drains, and that we would simply stick something in the drain holes from above to loosen up whatever was clogging them. It worked.

I hadn't even realized it at the time, but I'm confident that my partner was worried about sailing alone and partly chose me because of my seafaring skills. He had a lot of respect for me. For whatever reason, I was the one putting myself in the inferior position when I was around him. And I'm someone who is all about equality in the trades and celebrating female mariners! This experience helped me realize what my real weakness was: devaluing myself.

"Our doubts are traitors, and make us lose the good we oft might win, by fearing to attempt." (Bloom. H, 1987)

The Locks of the Welland Canal

Story by Jane Woo

As a sailor, you never know where the job can take you or what sights you will see. Every trip, every patrol, is different and can leave you astonished to say the least. A lock on a canal can help your ship sail from one body of water at a lower elevation to another body of water at a higher elevation. I have always found this fascinating.

When I was a little girl living in Hong Kong, I used to go with my grandfather down to the docks and watch the container ships load and unload. I knew I wanted to be a part of that, so when we moved to Canada in 1994 I knew I wanted to be a sailor. In 2008, I started a program at BCIT Marine Campus to get my Mate's ticket to work on big ships. I had to do 12-months of sea time as a cadet, during which I worked on container ships on the Great Lakes.

I enjoy the challenges of my job. Every day is different. I normally work two-three months at a time with one month off. The thing I hate the most about my job is that you can't just call in sick when a job needs to be done. I work four-hours on, eight-hours off, four-hours on, so it is hard to get a lot of sleep onboard. After months of this, you become exhausted by the end of a trip.

The Welland Canal is a very useful, very popular canal located in Ontario, Canada. It connects Lake Ontario to Lake Erie. The purpose of the Canal is to allow cargo ships from

Lake Ontario, which is at a lower elevation than Lake Erie, to slowly climb up through the locks to get to Lake Erie. It takes about 10-12 hours to go through all eight locks up the canal, which is about 27 miles long (43 km).

To go through a lock, the ship must be tied up on one side with wire ropes to prevent it from hitting the side of the lock. There are two mates on deck manning two wires each. Before going through the lock, the Welland Lockmaster tells you when it's your turn to go and operates the gates at each lock. Once inside the lock, the lock is then flooded with water to raise the ship up to the next lock, on average between 43-49 ft. The last of eight locks only rises a few feet to meet up with Lake Erie. A ship is not allowed to go into the locks during extremely bad weather.

When going through the locks, the drivers during rush hour are not at all happy when the bridge must lift every time the street lights turn red. All along the Welland Canal there are about eight locks with bridges overhead that must lift every time a ship goes by. There is also an observatory that tourists and observers can go to watch the cargo ships sail past.

Summertime on the Great Lakes is so peaceful and calm. You get the odd wind blowing out over the lake but on average it is mild. In the wintertime, it is too cold and 60% of the lakes freeze so ships cannot sail out over them. I normally get five months off during the winter, as my ship doesn't do much sailing. I don't mind as I can relax and do some travelling on my off time, maybe even go home to Vancouver to see my family.

I hope to be able to go to sea for as long as possible. I am just at the start of my career, and hope I have many more years to come sailing the locks of the Welland Canal.

Jane on the bridge of her ship-Photo courtesy of J. Woo

Life in Matzatlan

Story by Sandy Hill

You never really know where you will end up in life. I never thought I would be divorced at 40, looking for an adventure, and trying something completely out of my comfort zone. About seven years ago I started working as a deckhand for a company off the Coast of Mexico that chartered an 82ft. Schooner Staysail Sailboat. I never had any official training, but on the job, I've become versed in reading charts, navigation, basic deck skills, and astronavigation.

That little schooner saved me as a person. I put a lot of blood, sweat and tears into her, so I guess she will always be a part of me. The Captain built the ship in his own backyard in 1997. It took him six years to build it from Douglas fir trees cut down from his own backyard. He made it from different pieces collected from around the world; the portholes were from a tugboat built in 1892. The first time he sailed it, it didn't have an engine. They had to rely on sail. There were 14 other bunks and only one head (toilet) which made things difficult at times. We all slept in the cargo hold which was where the bunks were all located.

As a deckhand, I did everything from steering the ship, hoisting the sails, and maintenance, to cleaning the heads on board. I didn't care what I did, I loved it and still do. I was born and raised on a ranch, so I was never afraid of a little hard work. Although sometimes, it felt that as a woman I had to work a bit harder than everyone else.

I spent a summer back home in Virginia, USA, working on a Gaff Rig Schooner teaching kids about boats and how to sail. I later moved to Matzatlan, Mexico, where I have been working back and forth and am currently now living. I love the close-knit crews, but a lot of the Mexicans find it difficult to take orders from a woman. I am currently working four jobs that include freelance writing, teaching English in Mexico, teaching sailing, and sailing myself. My favorite part of sailing is the night watch, when I get to see the sun rise and set out on the horizon. There is also something completely magical about seeing the tiny phosphoresce in the water, and the millions of tiny stars up in the night sky.

I can remember distinctly when a mother whale breached out of the water giving us a warning for coming too close to her and her baby. She must have just given birth, as her baby was struggling and learning how to breathe. I just watched in awe, Mother Nature at her finest.

I still go to sea on occasion. I don't think I can really be away from it for any length of time. Sailing saved me in many ways, gave me a purpose in life. The ocean is both my passion and my new-found love.

Sandy looking over the side of the schooner

-Photo courtesy of S.Hill

Picture of the schooner from the bow

-Photo courtesy of S.Hill

The Walls Have Ears (and Eyes)

Everyone who works on a ship knows that you are working in tight quarters. You don't have much personal space, and if you are lucky to have your own space you have your own bunk in a tiny cabin. Unless you are an Officer, or the Captain, you usually must share quarters with one or more people on board the ship.

Everyone is vulnerable. Everyone sees you at your best and at your worst. It's not like working in an office where you only see your co-workers for eight hours. On a ship, you are with the same people for weeks, if not months, at a time. There are no closed doors to hide behind so to speak.

You see your fellow crew members in their uniforms, in their pajamas (or other night wear), in their civilian clothes, with make-up, without make-up, on good days and on bad days. You learn more about your fellow crew members then you probably ever want to know about them, but because you live so closely with them they become like family to you.

There are no secrets onboard. If someone spreads a rumor, guaranteed the whole ship will find out within 24 hours. I didn't even have to tell everyone I was pregnant with my first baby because I told one or two people and they did the job for me. Even your dirty laundry isn't safe from prying eyes, literally and figuratively speaking. If you leave your laundry in the dryer for too long, someone will move it, so they can do their laundry and there is no guarantee that they won't see your bras, underwear, or other night attire.

There was once a bra left in the laundry room that someone forgot to pick up and one of the guys went around asking every woman onboard if it was hers. How embarrassing. He was convinced it was mine, but it was about two-three sizes too big, I told him with confidence it wasn't mine, thank goodness. Even if it had been mine I don't think I would have been publicly announcing it.

These are only some of the issues sailors endure. When you finally get that cell phone reception you have been dying to get all month, so you can talk with your husband or boyfriend and realize the person next to you can hear every tender word you speak, it gets a bit annoying after a while. I once started receiving personal e-mails from someone's wife on the ship's e-mailing system by mistake and found out what her nick name for him was, oops. There is absolutely no privacy when it comes to certain things. If you leave your Facebook account open on the ships one and only computer, guaranteed one of your crazy crew members will post something cruel.

Men notice when women are acting a bit crazier than usual (especially during that time of the month) and when they are perhaps extra moody and irritable. You can't hide anything from your fellow co-workers when you work alongside them day in and day out. When a crew member is having a rough go with his or her home life, it's hard because everyone knows about it. If a wife is leaving her husband because he's never there, you know about it. At times, you can feel like you are in prison with nowhere to go by being stranded on a steel ship in the middle of the ocean. Some sailors even go "stir crazy" until they get shore leave to balance them out a bit.

I loved to be in my pajamas when I wasn't in my uniform and steel toed boots. Everyone and their dog knew what my pajamas looked like, knew what color my fuzzy slippers were and that I slept with stuffed tigers at night because I was homesick. I didn't care. When I wasn't on watch working, I was "home" not at work. That's how I relaxed.

My boatswain would often come to the crew's mess at breakfast time in nothing but his robe and a coffee mug in hand. He didn't leave much to the imagination, and didn't care what anyone else thought of him for doing it. I probably wouldn't have been so brave but who was I to judge when I walked around in my pajamas?

We all had to share the communal space. We all had to respect one another and make it work. We didn't have a choice.

It's especially difficult when you are not the one choosing who is on that big steel ship with you. You don't get a say and you must accept those people no matter what. They usually end up becoming as close as family members anyways as you really get to know someone on board. You always knew that at any time any one of them would have your back if you needed them to, especially when you are "up a creek without a paddle", so to speak.

A lot of budding relationships are created in a ship environment. It would be hard not to connect with someone as you work so closely with everyone on board, Blaine and I met on the ship ten years ago and have never looked back. Our strong friendship prior to dating was a good base for a loving marriage.

For the longest time before I met my husband, I always said I was married to the sea. No man could compare to the love I felt for the ocean.

I still have a love for the ocean of course. I will always love the smell of the salty sea air, wind on your back, that moment when you realize no one is around you for miles, but it's not the same as having my husband's love.

Sailboat Racing

Story by Heather Lee

Learning to put fear aside in the face of adversity is something every sailor must do in their lifetime. Fear hinders us physically and impacts our way of thinking. When critical situations arise, it is important that we can overcome those emotions. As one of my favourite dinghy racing coaches once told me, "Fleet leaders are sailors that have learned to anticipate and prepare rather than react and respond."

The way that I found my love for sailing was entirely a fluke. My mom put me in a two-week beginner sailing course to accompany her co-worker's daughter that had just moved to Victoria. At 11 years old, I was nerdy, and introverted with a bordering-on-unhealthy obsession with the *Lord of the Rings* (Tolkien, J.R.R., 1954-1955) trilogy. My mom was hoping that an unfamiliar environment might help me break out of my shell. On the first day of the course, (at the time, it was called White Sail I-III, now comparable to CANSail levels 1&2) the albacore dinghy that we were sailing in capsized just off the docks. Albacores, like all dinghies, are designed without the heavy keel that keeps keelboats upright. When a dinghy flips, it can be righted again using body weight as a counter-balance on the centreboard or the dagger board. Unfortunately, albacores also fill with water when capsized and need to be bailed out after they are righted. The girl that I was doing the lessons with was traumatized by the ordeal and never came back. Although my mom told me I didn't have to continue with the lessons, I had found the whole experience somewhat thrilling. I was hooked!

I begged my mom for more lessons and by the end of summer, I joined up with a sailboat racing team. I have pursued that passion ever since, but I'm still partial to the occasional *Lord of the Rings* (Tolkien, J.R.R., 1954-1955) marathon, extended editions of course.

In addition to racing sailboats, I have also done quite a bit of coaching over the years. I have taught four-year old's how to sail together in Opti Wet Feet, all the way up to coaching other racers at regattas. There have been many memorable moments in my coaching career. One that stands out to me occurred several years ago. I was teaching an adult intermediate class in lasers (a very popular one-person dinghy). I had checked the weather before-hand, and considered cancelling the day entirely due to the expected 20+ knot winds. I asked my head instructor if I could take the class as a group on a 23ft. Sonar keelboat we had. He said yes and both myself and the other instructor, Eric, thought it would be a neat experience for the class. Eric, was a more senior instructor than myself and insisted that we shouldn't put a reef into the main sail until we left the harbor. This is so the sailors could experience the heel and hiking out from the sail. In simple terms, putting a reef in the sail makes the sail shorter to reduce the power from the sails, and therefore decreases speed and heeling (the amount that the boat leans over) in breezy conditions. As we left the harbor I suggested the reef again to Eric, but he was insistent that we were handling it. As I watched Fisgard Lighthouse slip into the distance I thought to myself that I could feel the boat groaning as the bow slapped down over the rising waves. The Sonar had not seen regular maintenance for several years, and was in less-than pristine condition. Unbeknownst to anyone on board at the time, the deck had water damage and several weak spots, including an area surrounding the chain plate of the starboard shroud. As a large gust hit our sails I released the traveller to quickly dump the wind from our sails, but it was all too much for the boat to handle. Suddenly, there was a loud bang and whizzing noise as the starboard shroud sped past my face. I watched in shock as the mast sheared off at the deck and plunged leeward into the icy waters outside of Esquimalt Harbor.

In that moment, time passed very slowly, and I recalled the teachings of one of my very first keelboat skippers. Funny enough, at the time when he was instructing the crew on how to handle a dismasting, I felt his preparations were well over the top. It was in preparation for Swiftsure, not the Vendée Globe! But I was wrong then, and I was so grateful for his wisdom now looking back. I quickly checked to see that everyone on board was okay and that no one was tangled. Thankfully, everyone was Ok. Next, to make sure the hull didn't have any holes. It didn't, so I counted our blessings once again. However, I knew that in the rough seas we had to quickly lash the mast parallel to the hull or punctures would be inevitable. The sail was quickly dragging the mast below the surface of the water, so I decided to cut a few halyards and lines to lash the mast to the boat. Untying them would have wasted precious time. I tried to remain calm to reassure the students, and attempted to make a lesson out of the experience for them. We briefly debated whether we should call the Coast Guard for help but since the engine was working, and no one was hurt, we decided to limp back to the docks under our own power. My boss wasn't very happy when we got back to shore, but considering there were no injuries, and that further investigation revealed that the deck was rotten, it was all okay in the end.

There are always risks involved while teaching on the water, to you and the students. Wind and waves can be unpredictable, it can be challenging to keep everyone safe, especially when they don't listen to instruction. About a year after I started instructing, I taught this student, Abby, who was about 13 at the time and tended to be more defiant and dramatic. I was out in the powerboat alone myself that day coaching five 420 sailboats (named because they are 420cm in length), each with two sailors onboard. The volunteer who was supposed to be with me had gone home sick, but it didn't seem like an issue on such a calm and sunny day. The class was doing a drill called 3, 5, 7 which focuses on tacking and jibing between two buoys. As I scanned the harbor for any oncoming boats or dangers I spotted a line squall heading directly towards the sailors. I used a whistle signal to tell the dinghies to take their sails down and quickly moved boat-to-boat to offer any assistance. When I arrived at Abby's boat she insisted that her sail did not need to come down. I instructed that she observe the squall and listen to instruction, as I moved on to assist another boat that had a jammed main halyard. I looked over my shoulder to see if her boat had complied, but instead saw Abby sitting on the centreboard housing with her arms crossed, mainsail still at full mast. To my horror, as soon as the halyard was free on the boat I was helping, the line squall hit. I watched helplessly as Abby's boat capsized, hurling the two girls into the water. Although it was a warm summer day, the waters around Victoria are on average no warmer than about seven degrees Celsius, cold enough for shock to set in. Abby's crew mate quickly popped out of the water, grabbed onto the capsized hull and said she was okay. I quickly scanned the water for Abby. She was nowhere in sight. I called her name, no answer. Her partner knocked on the hull (there is an airpocket on the underside), but still no reply.

I was by myself in the little powerboat, so I thought to myself, "What do I do? Do I leave the boat and dive in after her?"

I visually checked the other boats one last time, and threw a little sea anchor overboard, so that my boat wouldn't float away. I dove into the water and swam up into the air pocket underneath the capsized vessel. Abby was underneath and breathing but in shock; she couldn't move her limbs. She was so frozen that I had to cut a couple of lines to be able to get her out and lift the lines around her arms. I grabbed a hold of her and brought her with me under the water to get free of the capsized boat. I ended up righting the 420 myself (and acquiring quite a few bruises along the way). Once the boat was upright and both girls were safely back onboard, I tied all five boats together and towed them behind the motorboat back to the docks. We talked about the dangers of hypothermia and the importance of preparedness to round out the day. I was glad that everyone was alright, and I hope that Abby learned a valuable lesson that day.

Throughout my years sailing I have competed in many classes including Laser Radial, 29er, 420, FJ and a variety of keelboats. 420 and FJ dinghies are similarly designed and are typically crewed by two sailors (this is called double-handed), both boats can be used for learning or tuned for racing. 29ers are also double-handed but they are designed for speed and performance, certainly a more advanced racing machine. Keelboats are sailboats with a keel. Most boats that you see tied up to a dock or moored at anchor have a keel of some form that works as a counter-balance to keep the boat from capsizing. Believe it or not, sailing is a summer Olympic and Paralympic sport, with dinghy and keelboat racing fleets. During my time at the University of Victoria, I was a member of their race team and travelled across North America to compete at a collegiate level in FJ sailboats. In the past I have leased boats or been loaned boats to race with, but these days I mostly race keelboats in short round-the-buoys type races or longer distance overnight races on other people's keelboats. Although I studied biology in university, I currently work as a sail maker. I just couldn't stop chasing my dream to work and do what I love.

One of the greatest challenges that a young woman in the sailing community will be faced with today is doubt from experienced male sailors. Keelboat racing is still very dominated by men. To be truly accepted, a woman needs to be strong physically and sharp mentally, she also ought to let any rude comments and negativity roll off her back. In my opinion, the attitude towards women in sailing is shifting for the better, so don't lose hope from a handful of haters. When I started sailing lessons at age 11, I had no idea that I would create so many memories on the water. I have become more confident as a sailor and as a woman over the years.

Although nobody else in my family shares my passion for sailing, they have always encouraged my endeavors. My grandpa, who worked as a tugboat captain for many years, was one of my biggest supporters and I believe it was because he also shared a special bond with the sea. Sailing has taught me not to be afraid to take chances and to try new things. As the old saying goes, "You can not control the wind, but you can adjust your course and sails".

Heather roll tacking in an FJ during practice

-Photo courtesy of H. Lee

Heather at the helm of a larger sailboat
- Photo courtesy of H. Lee

Stuck in the Bilge

Story by Nathalie Elliot

When it boils down to simple anatomy, women are very different from men. Their mental and physical, strengths and challenges, can somewhat differ. Sometimes, we can use this to our advantage and sometimes it can hinder us when doing the same job in a male dominated workplace.

My father was in the Navy, so I guess you could say it's in my blood. It all started when I was 13 and joined Sea Cadets. I trained until I was 18 and received my first marine engineering ticket as a fourth-class Marine Engineer. From there, I was an Oiler onboard a B.C. Ferry boat, later joined the Coast Guard in B.C., and then transferred to the Coast Guard in the Central and Arctic Region. I love being on the water. There is something about the challenge of being in the Engine Room that I adore.

I love the paycheck and I love the time off. It's hard when you are away from your family and pets, especially my cats, but it's worth it to have six months off a year to do with as you wish.

I have earned a lot of respect from my fellow shipmates, mostly because I "came up the haws pipe" as they say. Working your way from the ground up gains you a lot of hands-on experience, but there is value to having more book smarts. I have enough sea time to write my third-class ticket, unfortunately, I don't have the science background. You really need to put in the time and effort when you are climbing the ranks.

I spent a season on the West Coast of Canada sailing up to the Arctic on the *Sir Wilfrid Laurier*, but most of my time as a sailor has been spent on the Great Lakes. When we sailed off the coast of Vancouver Island, I never could have imagined the water being so blue. One night when I was off watch I was in the crane booth watching the phosphorescence on the windshield of the crane. It seemed almost magical with all the different colors covering the glass.

Ice breaking up in the Arctic is quite different from ice breaking on the Great Lakes. In the Arctic, you use the weight of the ship up on top of the ice to eventually break through the ice; on the Great Lakes, it's like using a hot knife to cut through the ice with the ship.

When I first started with B.C. Ferries, my orientation consisted of me, and two other guys who were applying for the oiler position. We were asked to figure out how to change the light bulb on a panel. The two other guys were trying to turn and unscrew the little cap on the light and it was getting them nowhere. I decided it would be easier to unscrew the panel and come in from underneath to change the light bulb and it worked! The coach leading the orientation was impressed and said his first kind words to me right then and there.

He said to me, "You are the only one who really knew what was going on".

This was after he had mentioned I should be on deck or applying for a catering position as he couldn't understand why I was applying to be an Oiler.

Some days it was challenging being a woman on a ship simply because of our anatomy. One day, I went to check the shaft seal between the deck plates of the bilge when I dropped a screw into the murky waters of the bilge.

I thought to myself, "I can grab it, no problem."

I wedged myself between the two deck plates and got into the small space, but when I finally grabbed the screw and tried to get back out between the plates I got stuck. My upper body strength is pretty good but when I tried to lift my body up and out, my boobs kept getting caught on the way out and I was officially stuck. I had to call out for someone to come and help me, how embarrassing.

I think my biggest challenge was getting my first assignment as an Engineer. I was posted on a 47' SAR boat and I was the only female onboard. This was more because it was my first time on my own without guidance, so I was worried I wasn't going to be good enough.

It was intimidating, and I constantly asked myself, "What have I got myself into?"

I had put in all the effort to get my ticket and had taken the initiative to learn on my own, so it all came down to that one trip. If I screwed up, they wouldn't hire me as an Engineer again; all that training, all that effort would have been for nothing. It was sink or swim for me. I didn't know what my full capabilities were until something were to happen.

I've learned that working on a ship is like being back in high school. Everyone gossips. You can't talk or trust anyone on a ship without him or her telling someone else without it spreading around to the rest of the crew. The saying is true that the "walls have ears" on a ship. You can't put up with anyone's crap, but it's best to take it with a grain of salt.

I will most likely continue going to sea until I retire. I may or may not have kids of my own, and I am quite ok with just being someone's crazy aunt Nathalie if it means I can keep going to sea. My husband and I have been lucky in that we are on the same schedule as he goes to sea as well. Hopefully we can continue having the same time off.

Recently I took on the job as Chief Engineer on a science vessel. Talk about a learning curve! I had a coupling failure and personal issues. I had new engineers rotating through and I'm also trying to learn a new ship. I have to say I'm not a fan of the paperwork but I'm glad I took the job. I've been making progress with the disrepair of the ship and I think I've been successful in keeping things together.

As for now, I have come to realize that women are just not the same as men. Sometimes we must adjust the way we look at things because we think, and problem solve differently or simply change how we reach for hard to reach items on a ship, so we don't get stuck!

Canadian Coast Guard ships tied up at the base on the East Coast

-Photo courtesy of N. Elliot

Nathalie in front of the ships propeller in dry dock
-Photo courtesy of N. Elliot

⚓

T.V Valour

Story by Capt. Laura Nelson

A single moment in time can change history, it can be so powerful and even change our destiny. When you are supposed to be somewhere but are not due to unforeseen circumstances or pure luck when tragedy strikes, all you can think is why.

Living in Florida, I live a somewhat enjoyable life. I currently work on IMR (Inspection, Maintenance, and Repair) boats that service Fourchon, Louisiana all the way down to the Mexican border. I work for companies like BP, Shell, and Chevron, and normally go to sea for 28 days or longer at a time. I currently work on *Ocean Alliance* that is 310' long, has accommodations for 69 persons onboard, and has a giant moon pool where we can deploy equipment. We launch ROV's (Remotely Operated Underwater Vehicles) over the side of the vessel with a LARS (launch and recovery system). We also have a helicopter deck onboard and have a satellite communications system for streaming live video and data from underwater operations.

I haven't always worked at sea. I was a bookstore manager for many years until I came across a book called *Do What You Love and the Money Will Follow*, so I did just that. I have always had a recreational boat and loved the water. I started my journey as a deckhand on a dinner boat and worked hard at my job. All my hard work paid off, and the port Captain then offered me a job on an inshore tugboat.

Women at Sea

Later, the ladies at Sea Sense Boating School approached me to come work for them teaching mostly women and couples how to drive and navigate their own boats. The instructors are all female and help women with the challenges of steering, navigating, and any engine problems that can all come with owning your own boat. I did an apprenticeship with them and still instruct on my time off from the big ships. I also do boat delivery where I sail a ship/boat for someone to a destination of their choice and they fly and meet me there.

I have been going to sea for the last 17 years, 12 years working and sailing in the Gulf of Mexico. In that time, I have seen and done many things and there have been definite "good times". There have also been a few dreadful times. Lives were even lost. What keeps me going through it all is a love for the solitude of being at sea. It makes you look at life and realize what is important.

I once did a delivery for a couple from Bellingham, WA to Astoria, OR on a 36' American Tug boat. We left Puget Sound and the weather was so bad that they had closed Grey Harbor Bar, which was exactly where we were heading. We had nowhere else to go and started getting low on fuel. I radioed the American Coast Guard to see where we could go, but there was nowhere else to pull into. They offered to escort us and of course I accepted the help. Getting stuck out in the middle of nowhere with no fuel would have been a recipe for a disaster.

If you're on the bridge, it is good to have medical training in case something happens to one of the crew members when you are out at sea. I was the Second Officer on the bridge one momentous trip when we were tied up alongside in Port Fourchon, Louisiana. I was lying in bed when one of the deckhands began pounding on my door telling me one of the Engineers had collapsed. They thought it was a heart attack. I quickly grabbed the AED (Automated External Defibrillator) and rushed to my fallen comrade. I checked his ABCs (Airway, Breathing, and Circulation) and found he had no pulse. We zapped him with the AED and briefly brought him back to life, but he later died on route to the hospital. If he had a chance of survival at all it would have been tied up at the dock, as we were so close to the hospital. If we had been out in the middle of the ocean it could have been hours until we got him professional medical attention. That experience changed me.

On January 18th, 2006, I had been working on a new ship and left my phone in my bag. When I returned to check my phone, I came back to a full voicemail box.

I thought to myself, "something must have happened."

I quickly checked some of the messages and found out that the Tugboat *T.V Valour* on which I had previously been working on had sunk in Frying Pan Shoals off the Coast of North Carolina. It was all over the news. My family and friends all thought I was still onboard. The tug had been on a journey from Delaware to Texas towing astern. It was fully loaded and got caught up in a storm. They were having stability issues with their ballast tanks. Three lives were lost that day; all friends, co-workers and adopted family members. The Chief mate, Chief Engineer, and an able seaman were among the deceased. One man's body was never recovered, one man died on route to the hospital and one man died of hypothermia. The survivors were lucky to be alive as it was one man's flashlight that saved them all in the pitch black of the night sky. If the survivors had been found any later than they were, they would have all died of hypothermia having no protection gear and no survival suits in the icy waters.

That incident really put my life into perspective and I know it could have easily been me on that ship. That day made me realize that life is short and to take full advantage of each beautiful day. I snatch up any opportunity that gets me back out onto the water.

I have been very fortunate through my career as a sailor, as I haven't had to pay for my certifications belonging to AMO (American Maritime Officers) and paying my yearly dues. Anytime I was in port I would sign up for free classes to better myself and get higher certification and eventually received my Chief Mate Unlimited Oceans license and DP unlimited. I will receive my Master Unlimited Oceans ticket this February 2018.

I will always be a sailor and continue sailing until I retire. You couldn't take me away if you tried. I do miss my partner and my dogs when I'm away, but I think I miss being away from the water more when I am ashore. One thing I would say to any woman wanting a career at sea is to strive to be the best you can be in your job. Learn your job and let your work speak for itself. Remember, life is too short to not do what you love. All it takes is one moment in time that can change your life forever.

Captain Laura on the helm
-Photo courtesy of Capt. L. Nelson

The Magic of Sailing

Story by Elize Duggleby

Sometimes you just need to open your eyes and see the magic and wonder in this world. From big to small it amazes me every day and makes living life worth every precious moment.

Now working as a Marine Engineer, I have my fourth-class engineering ticket. I grew up on the north coast, on Digby Island, near Prince Rupert, B.C. We had to take a tiny open skiff across the harbor to get to town and do our weekly grocery shopping, and basic errands. We took a ferry every day to get to school. My father was always involved with boats; he worked for B.C. Ferries for a time, then did fishing (salmon, halibut, and herring), and then later worked on tugboats. He built me a rowboat when I was nine, and when I was ten, he taught my sister and I navigation, how to use a compass, how to recognize buoys and beacons and what they meant, and the all-important rules of the road. I was always on the ocean growing up.

When I was 15, there was an event in the Atlantic called Tall Ships 2000. The Canadian government was sponsoring youth from across the country to go on legs of the trip on one of two tall ships. I applied and went for a week on the *Eye of the Wind*, from Charleston, SC to Philadelphia. It was the first time I'd really been away from home, and the first time I'd been sailing. It was magic.

The next year I went on another tall ship called the *Niagara*, where I volunteered as crew for the summer. I got back to school late that year after they gave me a paid job for the last few weeks, when the cook and the assistant cook quit just before a trip. It was great experience and I got paid to do something that I loved.

I came back and finished high school, I then accepted a job in the Arctic for a year as a cook and a first aid attendant in the mining exploration camps. I worked at a diamond exploration site in the North-West Territories and then finished the summer at an emerald mine in the Yukon. I had some money saved up, and no work for the winter (the operations up there are seasonal) so I answered an online add for a sailboat belonging to a German family that needed crew to help them sail across the Pacific Ocean. The vessel was called the *Infinity*, and at the time it was just a family with three kids, an unfinished boat that was a work in progress, and half a dozen volunteer crew, mostly who had no previous experience sailing. It was an experience.

I was born and raised on an island. I've been going to sea, all my life. I started a career at sea because it was a natural thing for me to do. At first, I was in love with sailing, the magic of the wind in the sails, the quiet of being at sea, watch keeping at night, under the stars, and the thrill of travel, of exploring, the freedom of traveling under your own power and being the discoverer. Now that I work on the ships, it's the time off that keeps me there, and the fact that I don't have to go in to an office every day. The fact that I work with my body and my brain, troubleshooting, figuring out the puzzles, and physically working on machinery. You should love those things to want to work down in the engine room.

That said, an engine room is not always a pleasant place to be. I remember being in dry dock on a cruise ship in the Caribbean with hundreds of contractors everywhere. It was complete chaos in the engine room with no air conditioning and grey water raining down on us every night while we were on watch. There was also no water to shower in as they were working on the pipes at night. There were emergencies every day when the ship blacked out, and being woken up at

8:00am in the morning by needle gunning on the hull near my cabin, after having worked until 4:00am was awful. It really was a dry dock from hell.

Sailing brings me closer to the magic of the natural world, seeing whales and dolphins, sometimes in massive groups of hundreds spanning to the horizon, sometimes so close I was able to reach out and touch them. I also love getting to travel and see places such as the pyramids at Giza. The pyramids are right on the edge of the city. That was so surprising. You see them between skyscrapers when you approach the city. Scuba diving in Fiji was amazing. I loved it. There were so many different amazing corals, tropical fish, and many sharks.

If you don't get along with the people you work with, you're stuck dealing with them day in day out for weeks or months at a time. It can be lonely. And it can be hard to get exercise in your daily routine if you're on a smaller vessel and the weather's bad. It can sometimes be rough for weeks at a time. I didn't like not being in control of what I ate on the ship. I like to cook and find it hard not to be in control of what goes in my body. Staying upright and in one place when the ship's pitching is another challenge, not to mention trying to sleep when your bunk feels like it's actively trying to throw you out of it. Getting enough sleep on a watch keeping schedule is next to impossible, especially while at sea for months on end.

When I was working on the cruise ships it really varied a lot with the crew I had. Some accepted me for who I was, and some didn't. It was always a bit weird for most of the guys to see a woman in the engine room, but most of them would come around and accept me after a while. I was part of a technical crew of about 100, made up mostly of Filipino and Indonesian crew members. The officers were mostly Italian and English. The crew usually liked me, because I treated them the way I treat everyone. Not all the officers treated the crew as equals, especially if they were different nationalities.

There weren't always women onboard the ships I worked on, except for the cruise ships. Only once did I have another woman in the technical department. We were both cadets and had to share a cabin.

As far as I know right now, I will be staying at sea working as an Engineer as my long-term career. I didn't get this far to throw it all away. The sea is a part of me and it will always be my magical place.

Elise working on the ships Oil Purifier

-Photo courtesy of E. Duggleby

Man! I Feel Like a Sailor!

While living on board a ship, you may find different scenarios and different perspectives from various women that can catch you by surprise. You usually work for eight-twelve hours out of the day, and the other hours are yours to do what you like. However, if you are on a vessel where the crews can consume alcohol (depending on what ship you are on) on their time off, colorful situations can occur. Whenever alcohol is involved, things invariably get out of hand. The fact of the matter is, it does not matter whether you are drinking or not, you are still at work and should keep a professional tone and manner.

As a woman, you need to fight for your right, prove you deserve to be there, and not make a name for yourself for all the wrong reasons. Work is tough enough for women in a predominantly male workplace. There are still men who don't exactly like women moving in on their territory and go out of their way to make it extremely hard for women to do their jobs. Some old sea dogs are set in their old ways and still think even to this day that women are bad luck on board ships.

I tend to disagree, but that's just my opinion. Like most women who decide on a career at sea, I believe we have just as much a right as men do to try our luck at being sailors. Why can't we do something that we love to do? Why can't we travel the seven seas and travel the coasts of our beautiful country and beyond? No one should be able to stop us. No one should tell us what we can and can't do. Whether we choose to sail until we retire, or decide to start a family and become stay-at-home moms, the choice should be ours. Our lives are our own.

I didn't care that some of the men didn't like me or didn't want me on the ship. I had the right to work in the profession of my choice just like any other Canadian citizen. It wasn't their choice to make. I followed my passion and had a blast doing it. If you have a dream you should go for it, and be happy. If it's not what you had expected, at least you tried and won't have any regrets later in life.

That is my life's motto: "No regrets. You only live once!"

I always had a strong connection to the sea. It's what makes British Columbia so beautiful. No one could take that away from me. No one. Who knows? If I had stayed going to sea maybe I would have ended up becoming a captain of my own ship. Just keep in mind that you can do anything you put your mind to it if you work hard to get there.

The women in this book are living proof that it can be done.

A Sailor's Chance

Story by Girija Edwards

Some people always know they have chances in life, although they might not know what they are at the time. Whether it be a new chance at love, a new career, or a new home, you can always find excitement and wonder in change.

As a Marine Engineer I am proud to hold my fourth class Marine Engineer's certificate from Transport Canada. I started in the marine industry when I was 42 years old as a deckhand on a B.C. Ferry in Alert Bay and worked there for four years. One day I peered into the engine room, a chance came for me to work in the engine room and I went on to pursue a career in Marine Engineering. Studying at the BCIT Marine Campus in North Vancouver, and completing a three-year program. It actually took me five years to gather enough sea-time to achieve my certificate.

I have always been a free spirit with real passion for healing and helping others like my father, Dr. Phil Edwards did. He was a tropical disease specialist who came from a prominent family in British Guiana. He and several of his siblings came to study at New York University. While studying at NYU, my father became a world class athlete. As a British subject he was to represent Canada in the Olympics as a middle distance runner in,1928, 1932, and 1936 Olympic Games, won five Olympic medals for Canada plus held the record for the most Olympic medals won by a Canadian athlete. The record stood for sixty four years! At the same time he was studying medicine at McGill university. My father and his brother were the first two men of color to be accepted into McGill University. Both graduated with honors in medicine.

My mother was a Scottish woman from the Isle of Wight. In Canada in 1943, it was not as liberal to accept interracial marriages like my parents. Both my parents' strength of character saw them through many rough times and through the other side to brighter days. I believe this is where I was given my confidence to do and go where I wish. Where my free spirit came from.

Since childhood, it was my mother's influence that allowed me to stay and live healthy using natural foods, a good lifestyle, classical Yoga and later Ayurveda (the ancient medical system of India.) This would be the foundation to maintaining my health and sanity in a world where women are never seen.

Therefore finding myself perusing a marine engineering career, as I did, seemed a bit contradictory. But to be fair, my mother's family were mostly deep sea mariners. Sea Captains and Commanders in the Royal Canadian Navy. My grandfather, Captain Archibald McDonald, was the last captain to sail a working Tall ship here on the Pacific Northwest coast and was the Harbor Master for Vancouver and later Esquimalt, British Columbia. For me, a Marine Engineer or anything nautical was furthest from where I seemed to be heading on my journey. Always running on my own time and never thought I would be working for anyone else, let alone a big corporation. When I first started with B.C. Ferries, I received my official uniform, an attire that was the complete antithesis to who I was, and I began to cry. I didn't really know what I had got myself into. The strict schedule and almost paramilitary style code of conduct wasn't exactly my cup of tea.

You could never be late for work. A boat was not a stationary site. If you missed the boat, literally, it would not wait. You do not sleep in. Two, at times three alarm clocks was not uncommon amongst marine crews accoutrements.

Initially, I had several nightmares in which I saw myself at the edge of the dock, watching my boat sail away. I would awake in a panic then see the three alarm clocks still set. If a mariner did miss their sailing, a crew mate may be forced to work another few hours at best and maybe a few more weeks or months at worst, as it is illegal to sail a ship without the full complement of qualified mariners. This is life in the marine world.

Becoming a female engineer was most unique. At the time, they did not exist. I later came to know I was, one of five women in Canada that held a Marine Engineers certificate from Transport Canada. This world was so foreign and male dominated that I had to quickly learn to navigate, not through waters, but through a myriad of big personalities. Holding strong with my personality, the opportunity allowed me to become part of a special team, that few people, men or women, get to experience. The complete inner workings of any large ocean going vessels, anywhere in the world.

As there is a global shortage of marine engineers, I have met people from every part of the world. Many wish to be in Canada working with the British Columbia Ferry Corporation. The move away from deep-sea life allowed mariners to see their families more easily. Months away at sea is not conducive to family life, no matter how lucrative.

I learned much more than just my engineering trade. I have honed my skills as a communicator with those whose mother tongue is not English nor their culture Canadian. It was a tool more important, most times, than the tool that hung on the rack.

Being a woman, especially a woman of color, and working as a ship's engineer in a man's world could have made it a challenge. Instead, it made me thrive in a challenging environment. I worked hard and had complete respect for the Marine Engineers I worked with. I soon came to know the skills, knowledge, and camaraderie, they possessed. The most surprising, for me, was the willingness to help me learn the complexities of the marine world below decks. As a woman, I became one of the guys. My first time working as an Engine Room Assistant (ERA) I was an extra helper. Quite truthfully it was my own test, to see if I could actually handle the intense and daunting task of large ship maintenance repairs and being on a watch. At a large dry dock facility in Esquimalt, B.C., I landed myself on the *Queen of Tsawwassen*-Vehicles: 376 Passengers: 1,630 Crew: 27 Overall Length: 129.97 m Length: 122.22 m Breadth: 23.20 m Gross Tons: 9,304.0 Service Speed: 19 knots Horsepower: 8,500.

We had almost finished in dry dock and were getting ready to launch the ship back into the water. The Chief Engineer was showing a new engineer around to all the void spaces. Just as he opened a hatch, a sudden gush of water came out of the space. Someone had been sandblasting the ship's hull and inadvertently made a small hole in the hull.

Because we were still in "dry dock" mode, all the pumps were non-operational. If that wasn't bad enough, at that very moment, the switchboard in the main control room caught fire because of a faulty wire. To top it off, the CO_2 extinguisher didn't work. Finally, another fire extinguisher was found and we tackled the fire before it spread. We quickly put a makeshift pump together and started pumping the water out of the void space. From our actions and quick thinking, we helped save the ship.

For anyone wanting to pursue a career as a Marine Engineer, male or female, you must love mathematics, problem solving, be able to work well with people, be physically fit, quick thinking, and adventurous. If not, you will not last and or be miserable. All Marine Engineers whom I've worked with seriously loved their work, as I did. I am very grateful to share this unknown world of Marine Engineering, especially as a woman. On both accounts a rare chance.

Girija working down in the Engine Room on a B.C. ferry

-Photo courtesy of G. Edwards

The Heart Wants What It Wants

Story by Jack LeMaistre

Nothing can prepare you for the harsh conditions of the wind and waves crashing against your boat during a squall. Quick thinking, stamina, and focus, are vital when riding out any storm.

As a seaman/deckhand who loves travelling the world, I started my sailing career in Victoria, B.C., but my journey has taken me to several ports of call in the U.S (Hawaii, California, Washington), Mexico, Costa Rica, and most recently Nicaragua. I sail mostly tall ships and a Cal 26 sailboat.

I grew up in Pincher Creek, Alberta. The summer I turned 11, my mother piled my sister and I, along with our two dogs, into a car packed to the hilt with camping gear. We headed to Vancouver, B.C. where I could smell and feel the sea air before I even saw it. From the second I felt the ocean within me, inside my soul, I found peace. I found my place in the world and I knew that the sea was calling me. In my young mind, the ocean was the only thing that made sense.

I knew when I was older that I would move closer to the sea. It was like I was magnetized, and it kept pulling me towards the salty sea air. I left Alberta to attend photography school. I somehow ended up getting a comfy government job in Victoria, a "big girl job", where I was supposed to be responsible and I was making good money, but in which I felt stuck. Something was missing. On my lunch breaks I would often go down to the Inner Harbor and watch as people climbed aboard their boats. I yearned to sail with them into the unknown.

I wanted to travel and see the world. I had this romantic idea of leaving and finding my passion. I started my journey by up and quitting my big girl government job and went down to Oakland, CA. and proceeded to Aberdeen, WA. to train with the Grays Harbor Historical Seaport Authority(GHHSA). There I trained on a square-rigged tall ship for two weeks. I learned the ropes, literally: how to tie knots, rig the masts, read charts and how to navigate. I also learned the tedious jobs required of a deckhand, such as "swabbing" the deck and scrubbing toilets. I learned a lot in two weeks. My mentors asked if I would stay because it was where I was meant to be. They knew it and I knew it was where I belonged.

I ended up staying and sailing with GHHSA for three months, got rid of my apartment and packed my life into a backpack. I stayed on the ship so long I then became part of the ship's furniture.

One of my most memorable moments happened just off the coast in Southern California. The wind had completely died and the water was as still as a mirror you could see the ships reflection. We were having engine troubles and so without wind or engine power, we were at a standstill. We didn't have anywhere to be at any certain time, which was good because we were getting nowhere fast. All the crew then came and lay on top of the deck to bask in the sun and take advantage of what was given to us. I loved the quiet, the peacefulness of it all.

I love the solitude, when I'm onboard a boat. You hope that the sea will take care of you but know that it can turn its back on you in a moment. You must respect the sea. You must be kind to it, and in turn it will be kind to you.

Just outside of Playa del Coco near Costa Rica, I was on board a Cal 36 sailboat built in 1967. Our boat was in severe wind (25-30 knots) and for 48-hours straight we had to take turns at the helm doing watches. For four hours, we took turns getting pounded by the ship as it slammed up and down against the wild sea. I felt so sick that for the most part I was up on the deck holding on for dear life just to breathe the fresh air. At times when the ship was pitching badly, I would be at an almost 90-degree angle, practically standing while holding on for fear that if I let go I would fall into the water below. During that ordeal, we shredded a jib sail (we didn't have a storm jib on). We were still 10-12 hours away from our Port of Call when we realized our port lower backstay had tacked. It was pulling out of the deck and it got to the point where we were concerned we would lose the mast. We were trying to keep it together but if we had lost it, we would have severely drifted due to the strong currents. We might have never made it to shore like we did. Thank goodness it worked out and we fixed everything once we got to our destination in Playa del Coco. At a closer look, the backstay had started pulling out of the deck and the fiberglass of the deck had lifted with it. The damage was great, but we were back on the water in no time.

The thing I disliked the most about being on a smaller vessel and when I was on the Cal 36 was the fact that we didn't have a proper fridge/freezer onboard. There is an icebox that is supposed to keep things cool but when you are down off the coast of Mexico and even the water is warm it doesn't work so well. We were dangling drinks overboard and holding them in the water just to try and cool them down, but it was difficult at the best of times. Fresh produce would only last for a maximum of about two or three days because it would spoil.

I love a good thrill and I guess you could say that when I first thought of going to sea, the excitement of it all was appealing to me. I thought it would be more exciting than it was but there were times when you really had to think about what you were doing as it could leave you or the ship severely crippled.

I am currently residing in Leon, Nicaragua where I ended up after all my travels. It's been over a month since I have been to sea and I miss it every day. I am currently trying to find a job on a ship to make my way back to Canada and hopefully one day start a family. I will always have a love of the ocean and hope to continue a career or go back to a career at sea. I will always be a sailor at heart and know deep down that I can weather any storm life throughs at me.

Jack working aloft, sitting on the Topsail of a tall ship the *Lady Washington*

-Photo courtesy of J. LeMaistre

Women at Sea

Jack skylarking on top of the mast on one of the tall ships
-Photo courtesy of J. LeMaistre

Fishtailing in the Panama Canal

Story by Cynthia Thomas

Sometimes things happen for a reason, usually when we least expect it. As much as we want to convince ourselves that it is meant to be, sometimes we have no control over it and it works out better in the long run.

I started with the Canadian Navy reserves as a Naval Communicator when I was 17 years old. I did basic training as well as basic seaman training and started working summers on gate vessels while going to University. Most of the time I was usually posted to one ship called the *Port de la Reine*. I worked as a Naval Communicator for almost ten years and worked my way up through the ranks as Master Seaman. I loved my time in the Navy.

One of the many challenges I faced going to sea was that I got terribly sea-sick. It got to a point where I would think about what the best food would be to throw up. You would think that ice-cream would be easy on your stomach, but it feels like hot foam coming back up your throat. People tell you to eat crackers to settle your stomach but what they forget to mention is that you need to drink a lot of water because it's like throwing up chunks of clay if you don't.

Working on some of the vessels, I often had to share a cabin with several other women. The bunks were usually stacked three in a vertical line with the bunks side by side. I sailed with a friend of mine and our bunks were beside each other. In between our bunks there were "buggery boxes" so you didn't roll or touch your cabin mate. When we went to sleep we would just be staring at each other which, was kind of weird but you got used to it after a while. "Buggery" is an old British term for sodomy, usually between two men. There was an inherent homophobia back in the day to "stop" it from happening in the Navy.

I sailed an MCDV from the east coast of Canada around and through the Panama Canal. I flew back east to get the ship ready to sail, and then sailed it from Halifax to Victoria. Along the way we stopped in the Cayman Islands, Florida, Mexico, Panama City and a few other spots on the trip around.

Off the coast of Florida, we ended up sailing in between two hurricanes. The ship was damaged by the strong winds and rough seas. At one point, I was sitting down at a computer backwards (looking astern) and we were being tossed around so hard that one of the filing cabinets tore off the bulkhead and crashed into me. Luckily, I had my feet up and managed to push it away to keep it from crushing me. All the shelves in the fridges and freezers in the galley got torn off the bulkheads during that trip, making a giant mess down below. These are just some of the dangers of a life lived at sea.

After the damage to the ship from the hurricanes, we limped to Florida where they fixed us up good as new. We also spent some time in the Cayman Islands where I got to experience new things, including eating turtle, and feeding and swimming with stingrays on a shallow sandbar.

As we were coming through the Panama Canal, there was a giant container ship following close behind our ship. We were being pulled by four mules (a mule is an electronic winch used to guide large ships through the canal, named after the animal who was traditionally used to pull ships) along the narrow waters of the canal with a pilot onboard directing our Captain, as he had more local knowledge of the area. Somehow, someone from the port authority had told the shore workers to let go the lines on three of the mules by mistake. Our ship was only hanging on by one mule. Suddenly we scraped up against the one side of the canal and swung around crashing into the other side. Our "Buffer", also known as the Boatswain mate, yelled to get out the fenders and throw them over the sides of the ship.

I remember looking over the side of the ship. The water line was about two feet away from my face and the Buffer started yelling,

"Fuck the fenders! Hold on tight, we're going to hit!"

The ship hit the side of the canal yet again. We ended up doing some major damage to the ship at the port authorities' expense. We headed to Panama City and stayed a few extra days to inspect the damage. We had our own divers check out the bottom of the hull, then limped to San Diego and slowly headed back to our home port Victoria, B.C.

I loved my time on the ships, so I continued, and eventually ended up being full time Naval Reserves. I even went as far as signing up for regular force but later found out they wouldn't accept me because of my severe peanut allergy. I couldn't be a certain distance away from a hospital or a doctor. Plainly put, I couldn't be out in the middle of the ocean for any length of time anymore.

I had learned to live with my allergy and couldn't figure out why they would no longer let me sail. Everyone on board knew about my allergy and knew that I carried an epi-pen around in a little box on my person in case of emergency. They even knew that the jam in the fridge with my name on it was mine and absolutely no one was to use it in case of cross-contamination with peanut butter.

Unfortunately, that was the end of my sailing career. I was so upset when they had to medically discharge me but at least I received a form of compensation. When I look back on it now, I realize it was for a good reason and I couldn't see myself still being at sea with a husband and three kids.

I loved the quiet and the serenity of going to sea. I loved the smell of the salty sea air and the routine of it all. Working for the Navy was regimented, but I thrived in the environment. The sleep deprivation was hellish but now that I am a mom of three kids I look back and think, "Wow, that was nothing." Do I miss it? Of course, but I wouldn't change what happened for the world. I love my life and couldn't imagine leaving my girls for any length of time. Maybe one day when the kids get older I will go back, but for now this sailing story is at an end.

Cynthia working on board the *Miramichi*

-Photo courtesy of C. Thomas

Cynthia on the deck of the *Miramichi*

-Photo courtesy of C. Thomas

Saying Goodbye to the Sea

I am a sailor. More specifically a seaman/deckhand onboard a ship, ready to save lives and help people at a moment's notice. That is, until the unexpected happened: I got pregnant.

I guess you could say that I was somewhat ready to be a mother, as I was 24 years old, had a steady career and lived with the man I loved. But was I ready to give up my so-called career as a sailor and have a baby? Give up going to sea forever, or at least until my baby was in university?

Does a woman have to choose between a life at sea and being a mom?

For me it was an easy choice. I couldn't bear to leave my child with anyone but myself for any length of time let alone an entire month straight. Of course, I had to stop going to sea, if I had a baby at home.

My choice was clear to me, but for those women who do go to sea and leave your children at home, my hat is off to you! I commend you first, for getting back into the workforce after having a baby, and second, for being able to leave your families behind no matter what your situation. I know it can't be easy for any of you. So, here's to all of you woman sailors out there! I raise my glass (of wine) to you.

I chose home life. Every fiber of my being was ready for this, to make a change, a very big change in my life. There was only one problem; I still went to sea while I was pregnant.

Going to sea pregnant was probably one of the hardest things I've had to do in my life. I was about 13 weeks pregnant when I left home for my last patrol at sea. 28 days of pure discomfort. I was suffering from continuous morning sickness, dizziness, and quite often I was seasick on top of it all. It all became a bit of a blur at one point.

All of this was when I was working 12-hour days of 28 days straight. I was exhausted. I had no resources, no boyfriend for moral support, none of my family to help me get through it all, especially my mom and sister. I was a complete and utter mess, an emotional wreck to say the least. My hormones felt like I was on a rollercoaster journey through the Himalayas, and every time I smelled anything to do with the engine room or one of the heads, I felt like I was going to heave.

That patrol in January 2009 would end up being my last patrol and probably my most memorable. The first part was telling everyone on the ship that I was pregnant.

I knew I had to tell the Boatswain right away, so he knew and could organize my watch accordingly. Of course, I was nervous telling everyone because it was so sudden, and I wasn't exactly married so I wondered what the crew might think. I told the Boatswain (my immediate boss) first as soon as I stepped on board the ship and he put me on light duties right away. It wasn't too long before the rest of the crew found out. Rumors like that spread like a wildfire on a ship.

My first week back at work, we were tied up at a Nanaimo dock and finishing an Out of Service (OOS). It just so happened to land on New Year's, so we all got together in the lounge of the ship and had a big celebration. I started work at midnight, so I was working and couldn't do much anyways, but being pregnant made my night even more challenging.

I had fun nonetheless and the other women onboard the ship kept coming up and rubbing my belly. I think some of the guys were even doing it too. It was kind of fun getting all the attention. If people on board didn't know about me being pregnant, they certainly found out on New Year's Eve.

What a way to ring in 2009, at work, tired, and pregnant. I didn't even get my New Year's kiss from my now husband. I missed being with him so much it hurt, and I missed having him there for support. 2009 was going to be the beginning of an extraordinary adventure. I was to venture off into motherhood in six months and I was scared to death. Scared of what was to come, scared of what I had to give up, and scared of having to care for another human being. So much responsibility now rested on my shoulders and at age 24, I was now obligated to be more mature, make tough decisions, and be responsible for a little person that I created.

There were many times I felt like I wasn't good at my job because I wasn't able to do certain tasks while pregnant. I couldn't ride in the small boats, I couldn't do any heavy lifting, I couldn't use any harsh chemicals, you get the idea. There were also times I felt like some of the guys resented me because of the work I couldn't do, fell back on them. I really was trying hard to do a good job. I wanted people to remember me as a hard-working deckhand and not some slacker that got everyone else to do her job for her. It was very frustrating at times. That said, I wasn't about to endanger myself carrying my child just because someone thought I wasn't doing my job properly. My job didn't mean more to me than my family, or the wellbeing of my unborn child.

I wasn't allowed outside for the first few days because they were painting the outside of the ship with extremely toxic paint. Of course, I wasn't going to expose myself or my baby, so I happily obliged.

The ship was finally finished in OOS and we left the dry dock and headed up North, sailed up the West Coast, and hit some rough seas along the way. What was I supposed to do when I was lookout on the bridge and feeling sick? I tried everything from Bonamine (the doctor said it was ok to take while pregnant), to Gravol for pregnant women, to drinking ginger ale and eating crackers up on the bridge. Nothing was helping. I couldn't keep anything down for almost three days straight. That wasn't good for me or my baby. Even I knew that. I kept eating crackers to at least keep food in my stomach, but they were coming back up just as fast as I was eating them. I was miserable, I was sick, and I was tired. Tired from fighting my own body, tired of working, and already tired of being pregnant.

When we finally arrived at our destination it wasn't as bad. We were at anchor, so the ship didn't rock so much. That entire patrol, I wasn't allowed to go in the RHIB. I had to watch as everyone else got to go fast and feel the wind in their hair and dreamt it was me instead. It wasn't fair. I just stood at the davit waving goodbye, waiting patiently for the RHIB to return, wishing I could be out there with everyone else.

I was sad. This was going to be my last patrol and I couldn't even get one last ride in the RHIB, my absolute favorite part of the job. I loved the speed and the shear grace. Just you and the ocean, wind in your hair, the salty sea air in your face. I got to launch the RHIB whenever anyone went in the boat that patrol. One small victory.

The guys on the ship decided to throw me the first ever baby shower on the ship. It was so thoughtful of them and a total surprise! I was called to the crew's mess towards the end of my watch one day and, to my surprise, everyone was waiting for me. The cooks had made an ample number of appetizers, including handmade cupcakes iced with pink and blue rattles and baby bottles.

As soon as I walked into the mess I started crying. It could have been the hormones again, but no one had ever done something like that for me before. It was the sweetest moment. There was a diaper cake one of the other girls had hand rolled and put together herself with a bunch of creams and lotions for baby hidden inside. There were little sheets of paper with baby shower games on them carefully placed on all the tables. It was fantastic and well thought out! They all put together a placemat decorated with pictures of the crew, including one of myself, and they had all signed a comment or two wishing me well. Someday I will be able to show it to my baby.

It was entertaining watching grown men play baby shower games and eat morsels of food and tiny cakes. It was the highlight of my trip and a nice break during a miserable patrol.

There were times when I felt I wasn't going to make it to 28 days. Sometimes I felt depressed and even unsure of myself, as a person, as a woman, and as a sailor. I asked myself on several occasions if I was making the right decision, if I was ready for this huge responsibility that lay ahead of me.

On the days I was really depressed, I even had thoughts of suicide. I wanted to throw myself overboard and drown my troubles away never to be seen or heard from again. I'm not exactly sure why -- maybe it was the hormones, maybe it was the stress, or maybe the shear panic of everything going on around me -- but sometimes I just felt like I needed a way out. Like I was screaming inside my head with no one to talk to on the ship. Even though there were three other women on board at the time, they couldn't begin to understand what I was going through. None of them had experienced childbirth or the changes my body was now going through. I felt completely and utterly alone.

I just wanted to go home. I wanted to be able to see and talk to Blaine, have a shoulder to cry on, and talk to my mom or sister when I wanted support about my pregnancy and the many changes my body was now facing. Not having that lifeline was detrimental to my health. As supportive as most of the guys were on the ship, they still couldn't fully understand what I was experiencing or what I was going through from day to day. I felt like I couldn't talk to anyone and at times would just shut down in my cabin, cry, or both.

I knew I had to get through it, for myself and for this tiny treasure I was carrying. I knew I would have felt like a failure if I had given up and asked to be sent home. I had to get through the last portion of the trip as hard as it was. I had to be careful, and I couldn't over exert myself. My job could be stressful and sometimes very dangerous. Regardless, I did love it and I was going to miss the excitement of going to sea.

Diaper cake and cupcakes provided on the ship at the baby shower

-Photo courtesy of B. Snider

I managed to get through that month at work. It was tough, but I survived, barely. I ended up taking a few months off on sick leave before I gave birth so at the very least, I didn't have to work on the ship when I was seven or eight months pregnant. If I had that much difficulty when I was only three-four months along, I could only imagine what it would have been like being three times as big and that much more miserable. It would have been hell on earth (or sea).

Walking off the ship onto the gangway and then onto the jetty for the last time was hard. It was emotional because I knew it was over. My life and my career at sea were now over. I may never go back to sea. Maybe one day my husband and I will buy a boat and get back out on the water, but it won't be the same. I had to say goodbye. Goodbye ship, goodbye crew, goodbye ocean, goodbye to my aspirations of becoming a ship's mate, or perhaps one day even a captain. Hopefully one day my kids can have an appreciation for the ocean. Hopefully it can be a big part of their lives as it was for me. The ocean has so much beauty and radiance to offer, for it not to be a part of their lives would be a shame.

Brianna looking out her porthole as she passed a lighthouse station near Nanaimo, British Columbia one last time

-Photo courtesy of B. Snider

Epilogue

The sea is a part of me. I will never let it go. I want to find out who I am, who I am supposed to become, and where I am going on this less traveled path. To go the distance and never let go of my hopes and dreams and to achieve something great.

I want to leave a legacy for my kids, for them to read about my challenges and share with them my triumphs as a woman in a male dominated work place, and as a sailor. For them to share with their family and pass it down generations for years to come and to say proudly, "my mom used to work at sea".

I want to be able to inspire someone someday to take chances and make mistakes. I want to live my life knowing I lived a good life, a different life. It is all possible, and for me it was a reality. There truly is nothing better than sitting on a beach watching the bustling movement of a busy harbor. The tranquility, the serenity of it. It makes me want to burst with joy and shout out to the world saying,

"I'm here, I am a part of this wonderful world."

From the tiny fishing vessels trying to catch a bite at 5:00am, or the kayakers waiting to catch a wave and watch the sunset over the clouds, to the larger cruise ships dropping off busy tourists wanting to explore a new land, every time I look out across the water something catches my breath, and when it does, every fiber in my being is at peace.

My heart yearns to be a part of it all again. What I wouldn't give to be a part of the excitement once more. I'm torn between being very career driven and being family focused. Balance is a hard lesson to learn in life. I admire and look up to the women in this book who have come so far in their careers and have done well for themselves going to sea. It was an absolute pleasure to interview every single one of these women and I acknowledge the bravery involved in coming forward and sharing their stories.

My hope is that one day this book might help another person either on the water or in life in general. Maybe you will have your own sea story to share one day. Whatever it may be, be creative, be inspired, and continue to dream.

Without our oceans, humans would not be able to survive on this earth. Please be kind to our beautiful oceans and other bodies of water, and all the wonderful creatures in them from tiny too big. Our own children and our children's children will thank us someday.

My husband and I try and incorporate the ocean into our everyday lives with our kids, watching them and helping them grow and see the beauty it can offer. From kayaking, paddle boarding, swimming, surfing or boating, we make every effort to engage them.

From my family to yours, we wish you all the best in your future sailing adventures.

Brianna Snider

Blaine, Sienna and Kohan smiling for mom on a family kayaking adventure in Brentwood Bay, B.C.

-Photo courtesy of B. Snider

To anyone seeking adventure and beauty, look to the stars to guide you and let the sun rising over the horizon show you the way

-Brianna Snider

So, you want to be a sailor, now what?

(Tips and tricks to help you get there)

The following chapters will help and inspire anyone who is serious about a career at sea. I have included my own personal experiences as well as the route I took to get there and some information on what you can expect. To get started, someone wanting a career at sea would first need to find out what she would want to do on a ship. There are endless possibilities to choose from. You can be a watch keeping mate/captain on the bridge, or a steward/cook in the galley. Some women are also deckhands/seamen or oilers/engineers. In the Navy, you can be a communications officer, technical specialist, aviation officer, and many other positions to choose from. It all depends on your interests, background experience, and what you feel you would be happy doing.

The decision to pursue a career at sea is certainly not an easy one for any woman. Ultimately, a woman must make the tough decision of whether she wants to make a life of it, or whether she wants a family or have children of her own. Of course, I am not saying if you want children at some point that you can never go to sea or work at sea, but your career will be short-lived if you decided to get pregnant and you may or may not want to go back once you have a family at home. Most women choose not to. There are a select few women who do end up going back to sea after having children and there isn't a right or wrong decision. It is a very personal choice based on different circumstances. Women that go back to sea after having children should be commended. It certainly would not be easy leaving for any length of time and being away from young children. For myself, I got pregnant while I was still working on ships and I couldn't bear to leave my daughter for any length of time let alone a full month. Priorities change, and circumstances change when you have kids. But then again, there are some women who don't have kids or who will never have kids and make going to work at sea a lifelong career. Some even go on to become captains of their own ships.

Keep in mind if you have never been to sea, or never been on a boat for that matter, there is also the possibility of getting seasick. Now some people don't get seasick and others get so sick they cannot even pick themselves up off the deck to make it up over the rail to spill their cookies. I happened to be one of the not so lucky ones and got seasick every time we were in any sort of rough weather. Not exactly the time of my life, that's for sure. I always had to have my trusted anti-nausea pills with me and I list some of my favorites in Anti-Nausea Drugs and Remedies (pg.183).

When dealing with anything to do with transportation, there are laws in place to make sure everyone is operating by a standard code. In Canada, the rules and regulations are set out by Transport Canada (In Canada), IMO (International Maritime Organization) and STCW (Standard for Training, Certification and Watch keeping) and issue certificates of competency that are recognized worldwide.

Every seagoing person in Canada must have a valid seafarer's medical issued by Transport Canada. This certificate deems them physically fit to work and live at sea. A licensed practitioner near you can do this for about $100 as of this year in 2018, and a list of certified doctors can be found on Transport Canada's website.

Depending on what job you choose, you are required to be certified with proficiency in survival craft as well as firefighting and marine emergency duties. These are two very extensive courses and are not for the weak of heart. You must know what to do in case of an emergency, as anything can happen while at sea. Your ship could catch on fire and unfortunately you can't call 911 in the middle of the ocean, so your crew must be trained to put the fire out. Your ship could be sinking, and you must know how to save it, or when it's too late, when to abandon ship. Overseas, you must also know what to do in the chance of piracy (no joke, except nowadays they carry AK-47's instead of machetes). The ocean is a big place, and for the most part, it is just you and the wood, fiberglass, or steel, hull that is going to either save you or kill you. You must respect the ocean, as it is one of life's most amazing, most destructive mysteries in this world. There are places in the vast ocean where no man has ever explored before at unknown depths. We all still have a lot to learn when it comes to the sea. It is a very powerful, very wild lion that can never be tamed.

I have listed some of the courses I took below to get my certification to become a deckhand. Most of these courses were part of the Bridge Watchman program I attended through BCIT in Vancouver, B.C.

MED-B1, which is called Proficiency in Survival Craft Marine Emergency Duty, this course is where you learn how to launch a lifeboat from its davit. When I did my course, we went out into the harbor and went for a boat ride. We all took turns and got to drive the lifeboat just to get the feel of how it handled. We got to take turns giving orders and practiced taking charge in some emergency situations. We learned what the different types of survival equipment were and what the national standards were for keeping this equipment up to date on your vessel. We were in the pool a lot with this course and practiced putting a survival suit on and off in a timely manner. We also learned how to respond in emergency situations, such as the importance of staying together in the water to make yourself better seen by your rescuers. We learned how to launch a life raft and how to pull the painter line to launch and inflate the life raft. One of the perks of being the only girl in my class was that my teacher let me pull the line to inflate the life raft in the pool.

We all got to board the life rafts and see what it was like inside. We took turns flipping over the life raft, then re-flipping it back right side up in the pool (Yes, we had to get into the water). It was scary because you had to use all your weight and pull back on the raft to tip it over, so you ended up going underwater underneath the life raft. You had to hold your breath for about 20 seconds underwater kicking yourself from beneath the raft making sure your limbs didn't get caught in the floating lines attached.

Even though we were in a safe environment, my adrenaline was still pumping, blood rushing to my head. It was good to get used to what it would feel like if you were stuck in a life raft during an emergency. Each life raft must be SOLAS (Safety of Life at Sea) approved, and are also equipped with water bladders, a first aid kit, emergency equipment such as flares, whistles, food, and seasickness pills, enough for the maximum amount of people allowed in the life raft.

We watched videos on different emergency situations that had happened in the past and what people could have done better in those certain circumstances to help us learn and grow from past mistakes. Some of the videos were heartbreaking and overwhelming. Over the years there have been many lives taken by the sea. You must know what the weather is always doing, including the state of the sea, and the location of your emergency equipment. Some lives have been lost simply because preventative maintenance or action was not properly taken.

MED-B2 or also known as Firefighting Marine Emergency Duty, was an especially difficult yet rewarding course. The first day was spent in the classroom, going over safety rules and information on how to fight a fire on a ship. It wasn't until later in the afternoon where we got fitted for our SCBA's

(Self Contained Breathing Apparatus) and all our firefighting equipment that we were going to be using throughout the week. This included our turn out gear, aka our firefighting uniform.

The firefighting equipment included: gloves, pants, jacket, helmet, balaclava, mask, and boots. I had to make sure my hair was tucked back into my balaclava. I couldn't have a single hair showing because it could get singed or light on fire when fighting close fires, no one likes the smell of burnt hair.

We learned how to use different types of fire extinguishers and what purposes they all had. We learned what a thermal layer was and what signs to look for when a fire was not safe to attack. We also learned about boundary cooling, which is when you have a team with a hose, cooling above and on the sides of the building or room where the fire is located to help control the heat. Proper ventilation is also key when fighting a fire, to ensure the firefighter doesn't get smoked out or barbecued like a chicken when attacking the fire.

Now, I had certain issues with this course. It is not a course for the weak, and for some reason one of my instructors did not like having a girl in his course. He made my life a living hell for that entire week. He picked on me and yelled at me several times over the course of the week. He made me cry the very first day of the course. To my credit, I have worn SCUBA (Self Contained Underwater Breathing Apparatus) before being a scuba diver so it wasn't like I didn't have a clue. I wasn't used to the ones they were using in the course as they had different connectors. Instead of instructing me, the instructor yelled at me in front of the entire class and said I would die in a real emergency. I think it was safe to say that everyone that was in the room watching this all go on said he was too hard on me and had it out for me from the get go. I had several guys come and check on me to make sure I was alright after class. This was just one of the many challenges I faced being a woman on my career path to become a sailor.

The other issue I had with this course was a big thing for me, it was that I had a childhood fear of fire. I used to have nightmares about being burned, and I couldn't even use a lighter or light a match until I was well into my late teens. I feared being anywhere near a fire and the course I was taking was a firefighting course. Go figure, huh?

It was all part of the certification process. It was one of the most challenging tasks I have ever undertaken. I had to face my fears and finish the course, so I could move on with my life and start my career as a sailor. It's not like I was going to be fighting fires as my career. This was simply "in case" a fire happened on board a ship. You can't call 911 when you are out in the middle of the ocean, you and your crew are the only ones who can save the ship when disaster strikes.

On day two we started putting small fires out with fire extinguishers. We had to go into a pitch-black room filled with smoke and practice getting people out of a burning building by way of our other senses without relying on our vision. When you are in a real fire there is usually no light and usually lots of smoke, so you are not able to see anything. We had to pull out 150 lb. dummies from the "burning building". Being of smaller build than most of the guys in my class, I managed by dragging the dummies out anyway I could.

They showed us different ways to get a person out without straining or over exerting ourselves too much. If the person is much heavier then you, there is a dragging technique, in which you grab the person under both arms and pull them, allowing their feet to drag. (They probably wouldn't appreciate you dragging them out with their head dragging on the ground). There is also a fireman carry, which involves throwing someone over your shoulder to carry him or her out of a burning building or boat.

Brianna spraying a fire hose during the MED-B2 course at the Justice Institute of British Columbia in Maple Ridge

-Photo courtesy of B. Snider

Another certificate I needed to get as part of my Bridge Watchman program, was my WHIMIS certificate (Workplace Hazardous Materials Information Systems). It was a course done by computer, comprised of approximately 20 questions in total. It was a run down on how to be safe in the workplace, what to do with hazardous materials, how to handle them, and what precautions to take with dangerous goods. Something all sailors eventually work with on a ship. Every chemical needs to be properly labelled and have an MSDS (Material Safety Data Sheet) located nearby, in case someone is exposed to that chemical by inhaling, skin contact, or ingestion. A MSDS sheet helps identify chemical properties and what to do in case of exposure to that specific chemical as all chemicals are different.

To be able to talk on the radio, I took the ROC-MC (Restricted Operators Certificate-Maritime Commercial) for talking on the VHF. This was a week-long course because it was one higher up then just the basic course. To work on a commercial ship, you need to have this one, so you can talk with other vessels and call for help if need be. The basic ROC course can be completed in a couple of days and you need to memorize the phonetic alphabet for both courses.

My absolute favorite course I took, was after I started working for the Coast Guard. They put on a RHIOT course (Rigid Hull Inflatable Operator Training) that helps train employees, other government departments, and other Coast Guards from around the world in the FRC (Fast Rescue Craft) in heavy weather (See pg.66).

Most of the courses were fun, exciting, and put me one step closer to achieving my goals of becoming a sailor. The above listed courses are basic and mandatory for most positions on a ship. You could go on to become a mate or an engineer with further training and education.

Packing for Sea

What to pack in your sea bag:

- **Clothes/uniform**-for all weather conditions.
- **Ample socks and underwear**-enough so you don't have to be doing laundry every other day.
- **Long johns**-for those long and stormy nights.
- **Flashlight**-most important item on a quartermaster's belt to walk around and do security/fire rounds at night.
- **Books**-there is plenty of down time on a patrol to catch up on your reading.
- **Soap/Shampoo**-you will need enough for one-two months.
- **Flip-flops for the shower**-you don't want to come home with a form of foot fungus. Yuck!
- **Special snacks**-snacks you can keep in your cabin that you can't go without for any length of time and that they won't be providing or selling on the ship. Chocolate bars or candy, beer, smokes, chips. If you are like me, chocolate is a necessity. I can't go more than a few days without my fix. If you're lucky you will have a canteen on board the ship to buy supplies.
- **Work boots or shoes**-they usually should be steel toed and be approved by the Canadian Standards Association (CSA).
- **A Knife/Leatherman**-this comes in handy for any sailor. I would recommend putting it on your belt, so you always have it with you in case of emergency.
- **A Marlin Spike**-for splicing line or rope.

What to pack for sea if you are a woman sailor:

- ⚓ **Enough tampons**-you never want to run out of these when you are stuck out in the middle of the ocean.
- ⚓ **Extra going out clothes**-you never know when you are going to be in port, so you might as well have a little black dress on hand.
- ⚓ **Toiletries**-shampoo, soaps, hand moisturizer for chapped skin, baby powder for your stinky work boots, toothbrush, tweezers to pluck your eyebrows, etc.
- ⚓ **Razors**-are optional, as for the most part no one will see your hairy legs. (Unless you get lucky one night)
- ⚓ **Bathing suit**-if you are in port and there are hot springs nearby or if you decide to go for a dip in the ocean. Disregard previous statement if you choose to do this.
- ⚓ **Shampoo and conditioner**-for your hair.
- ⚓ **Extra towel**-to dry your hair and washcloth or puff to scrub yourself with.
- ⚓ **Your favorite chick flick**-for a night when you need a good cry. Trust me you won't find a single chick flick on a ship full of men.
- ⚓ **Chocolate, chocolate and more chocolate**-a girl can never have too much.
- ⚓ **Romance novel**-and a stuffy for all those lonely nights.

Of course, all other items on the previous page apply as well.

What to pack in a dry bag for short trips in a small boat/vessel:

A dry bag is a waterproof bag that seals up watertight so your precious cargo it carries doesn't get wet. You can buy them pretty much anywhere that sells water sports equipment or even snowboarding/skiing equipment as it works for snow as well. You want to make sure your dry bag is big enough to carry the following items:

- **A bottle of water**
- **Snacks**-such as granola bars, fruit snacks etc. You want to be prepared if you run out of fuel or get stranded somewhere for any length of time.
- **A pair of warm dry clothes**-in case you fall overboard and start to get hypothermia.
- **Extra set of keys to your house or car**-in case you drop your other pair overboard and can't retrieve them.
- **Your cell phone**-in a resealable plastic bag to keep it nice and dry.
- **First Aid kit**-in case you or someone else injures themselves.
- **A waterproof camera**-in case you want to take pictures of the marine wildlife.
- **A silver thermal camping blanket**-you never know when it could come in handy if your freezing out on the water or if you or someone else gets hypothermia.

- ⚓ **Waterproof matches**-these come in handy for making fires ashore if you get shipwrecked and need to call for help, or cook your dinner.
- ⚓ **A flashlight**-with the batteries separate in a zip lock container.
- ⚓ **Local charts**-to keep on your person in case you get lost. If you are boating/kayaking/canoeing/or what have you, you should always bring local charts of the area.
- ⚓ **Gloves, and toque**-to keep your hands dry and stay warm.

Photo by Terrance Lam Photography

What to put in your Lifejacket/Life vest:

Everyone who is near, in, or around the water should at least have a lifejacket or life vest accessible. You want to invest in a good quality life jacket that will last you a few years. Keep in mind that the foam inside a lifejacket does break down eventually, especially if the lifejacket is not stored correctly and is exposed to the elements such as the sun, or if it gets wet and is not dried properly. You will have to test your lifejacket every year to make sure it still floats. (You can do this in the summertime so it's not as cold). Make sure when you test it, you wear all the clothes you would normally wear when boating such as jeans, t-shirt, shoes, etc. as to get the correct weight. (Raid your closets for clothes you don't mind getting a little wet).

Make sure there are enough lifejackets on board for each person and child on board. If there are kids, make sure you have the appropriate size life jackets (measured by weight) when heading out to sea. Here is a list of everything you need on your lifejacket:

- **Strobe light water activated-** in case you are unconscious and cannot activate it manually. A quick flashing strobe light is a distress signal on the water.
- **Flares hand held-**to attract attention to yourself if you fall into the water.
- **Whistle-**to call for help if you get in trouble.
- **A knife-**to cut free of netting, rope, etc. Make sure it's a dive knife with a blunt end if you are going to be on a rubber boat so you don't pop it by accident.

⚓ **A Waterproof VHF Radio-**so you can communicate with the boat/ship in case you fall overboard or need to go ashore for any reason.

Some of these things may in fact save your life one day so be sure to be diligent. A good sailor always prepares for the worst. Unfortunately, things happen out on the water and it's everyone's job to help prevent accidents and fatalities from happening.

Here is a picture of a good quality lifejacket with reflective strips on the shoulder and some of the safety equipment that you should carry.

Photo by Terrance Lam Photography

Anti-Nausea Drugs and Remedies

When you are a sailor you will come across some hefty seas. If you are anything like me, you will want to bring something with you and have it on hand for those rough sea conditions. Sea sickness is often more preventable then curable, but this is what I recommend:

- **Bonine/Bonamine (USA)**-this was my lifesaver, the only thing that worked without making my drowsy. I have been told, that it can make you drowsy though so be careful if you attempt to use this. It can be purchased over the counter in most pharmacies in the USA but is no longer sold in Canada.

- **Gravol**-this made me sick and very drowsy but again it works differently on different people. I have been told it works better on some people. This can be purchased in most if not all pharmacies.

- **Ginger pills**-this is a natural route and it comes in little capsules with ground ginger in it. This works as a preventative measure but not the greatest if you are already seasick. Other alternatives are Ginger ale, ginger tea, ginger gum or eating raw ginger. This can be found in most health food stores and some grocery stores. Just be careful if you've taken it too late and it comes back up, it burns!

- **The patch**-this little patch goes behind the ear and is supposed to work for up to three days. I've heard it works great. I never got around to trying it, so I don't know if it works or not.

- **The wrist band**-the wrist band is supposed to hit a pressure point on the back side of the wrist using acupressure to make your body not feel nauseous. This did not work for me but apparently it works for a lot of people and a lot of them are purchased every year.

One thing to know as a sailor, is that each boat/ship is different. Each one has their own movement and a different way the ship pitches and rolls. Different types of weather can factor in and affect you becoming sea sick. If it is your first time at sea be sure to bring something for it just in case because you don't want to be stuck in the middle of the ocean without it. The last thing your crewmates want is for you to barely be able to do your job and stuck heaving over the side of the ship.

On my very first patrol out at sea, I was once sick so bad that I couldn't even pick myself up off the deck to go to work. I was on the ship's wheel, steering and was heaving so bad that I needed a garbage can beside me. I literally wanted to throw myself overboard on several different occasions because I couldn't bear it anymore. It is the worst sick I have ever felt in my entire life. You have no control over your body, it can be painful, exhausting, and you wonder what you did to deserve this form of punishment.

Women at Sea

Photo courtesy of B. Snider

Brianna Snider

⚓

Rules of the Road

The most common rule of the road that almost everyone knows by heart is "Red right return". It means that when returning into port upstream into a headway, always keep the red buoy (also known as the starboard buoy) on your right side and you will be in the clear. See figure below.

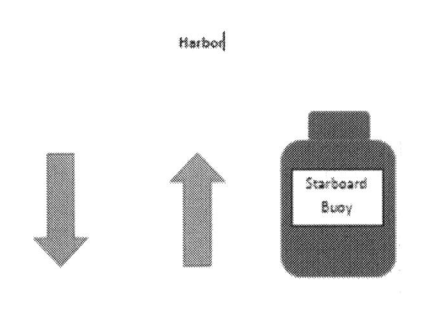

Harbor

⬇ ⬆ | Starboard Buoy |

**Red right return when coming into a harbor

There are all types of tricks to remember the rules of the road such as:

- **"White over red, pilot ahead"** - regarding navigation lights at night it, means a pilot vessel is ahead.

- **"Red over red, the old man's dead"** - regarding navigation lights at night, it means the vessel is not under command.

- **"Green over white, fishing tonight"** - regarding navigation lights at night, it means the vessel is engaged in fishing operations and to stay well away from it as it may have lines and netting out.

Number one most important rule of the road is "Always keep a good Look out

Second most important rule of the road is "Take action to avoid Collision". This one means, if someone is going to run into you, move out of the way to ensure there is no collision even if it's against the rules of the road. When you are trying to avoid one vessel, make sure you do not lose sight of other vessels that are around you.

For a full list of the rules of the road in Canadian Waterways you can go to Transport Canada's website and download a free copy of the Safe Boating Guide.

It is a good idea before you even step foot onto a vessel to have a basic idea of the rules of the road. If you will be driving the vessel at the very least, you need to have your pleasure craft operator's certificate (PCOC). You must pass a test to get your PCOC.

All too often, I have seen people stranded on the water because it got dark while they were out on a day trip and they didn't know what all the blinking lights meant or how to get back to their home port. One occasion I will always remember was when someone had just bought a new million-dollar sailboat as their new "toy". I guess they didn't get the MEMO about learning how to use it and learning the rules of the road before they used it. The very first time they took it out on the water, they ran aground by hitting a rock and puncturing a hole in the hull. You would think that if you spent that much money on a new toy, you could afford some sailing lessons?

Many people think that because they are on the water, the rules about alcohol don't apply. Like any motorized vehicle you are not allowed to drink and drive a vessel. In fact, in some cases they can take your driver's license away if you are caught drinking and driving a boat. You take the same risks getting into a boat with a drunk driver, they are putting the lives of the people in the boat in danger as well as the lives of people in other vessels. Why risk it?

So, please before you go out on the water, learn the rules of the road. Learn how to use a radio in case you get into trouble and need to call for help, and learn some basics on how to take care of your boat so you don't get stranded out there. The ocean is a big place and there will not always be someone nearby to help you.

Like I was taught in Girl Guides, always be prepared. You can never be too safe when it comes to your friends and family. Make sure you have enough life jackets on board for every person. Make sure you know where all your lifesaving equipment is located onboard and make sure you always remember safety first. I can't stress that enough.

Most importantly, have fun on the water!!!

Hierarchy on a Ship

You don't need a degree or diploma to work on a ship, depending on what you want to do. That said, to be an officer on a ship you do need to have a certificate of competency from Transport Canada (In Canada) saying you can work as an officer and have gone through the examination process. Here I will list the different positions onboard a vessel from highest ranking to lowest. Please note that ships will vary and the bigger the ship the more positions it will have. For example, the navy has six times the crew of a regular ship, and hence has more positions.

Captain (Master Mariner/Master Near Coastal)-highest rank in all the seven seas. Requirements are listed on the Transport Canada website listed under Chapter 10 Section 10.1 Master Mariner. The Captain oversees the entire ship and its company.

Captain/Skipper-in charge of the entire ship/boat and its company on a smaller vessel.

DECK:

First Mate/Chief Mate-they relay messages between the Captain and crew and oversee the deck crew. They command the boatswain who commands the deckhands/seamen. He also organizes the bridge team, rotations, discipline, supplies, etc. See Transport Canada Chapter 16 Section 16 for requirements.

Second Mate-oversees the night watch when watch keeping. Depending on the ship watches, some watches are 8 hrs. on 8 hrs. off; others are 12 hrs. on 12 hrs. off. When the ship is steaming at night, the second mate oversees the watchkeeping deckhands (or quartermasters) and gives orders to steer the ship and is responsible for safe navigation at night. The second mate is also in charge of charting upcoming trips. See Transport Canada Chapter 12 Section 12 for requirements.

Third Mate-oversees the day watch when the Captain or first mate is not available. The third mate is also in charge of organizing the muster stations including doing a full fire and safety gear inspection. A watch keeping mate certificate certified by Transport Canada is required. To achieve this, you need a certain amount of sea time as a quartermaster and deckhand to be able to write the exam.

Boatswain-is the immediate supervisor of the deck crew including deckhands, quartermasters, twine hands, leading seaman, and ordinary seaman. They organize the ship's husbandry and make sure everything is latched down and secured so nothing moves on the ship in a heavy sea. They are also in charge of any ship's activities/programs during the day for which deckhands or seaman are required, including tying up or letting go of the ship.

Leading Seaman/Able Seaman-the more experienced deckhands/seaman and get paid a little bit more. They are the ones who do more of the advanced jobs and guide the ordinary seamen when doing deck operations.

Ordinary Seaman/Deckhand-knows how to do everything on board a ship. From steering the ship taking helm orders from a mate, tying the ship up to the dock or letting go of the lines, general handyman work including: painting, chipping, grinding, doing routine checks called "rounds" to make sure the ship isn't on fire, to taking out the trash and recycling, they pretty much do it all. If something is broken, they fix it.

Quartermaster/Helmsman-as a quartermaster, you are a watchkeeper and in charge of being a lookout on the bridge as well as a helmsman (responsible for steering the ship). You need to have your Bridge watchman certificate of competency and know the rules of the road, navigation lights and buoys and can keep a sharp lookout for any dangers that lie ahead.

ENGINE ROOM:

Chief Engineer-is the highest position below decks and oversees the entire engine room department. They only take direct orders from the Captain or skipper him or herself. The "Chief", as some people refer to him or her, often does most of the paperwork required in ordering parts and regarding safety equipment. The Chief makes sure the first (senior), second and third engineers do their jobs correctly and that they oversee their oilers accordingly. Chief engineers will rarely put their coveralls on and get "dirty" so to speak. Overall, they oversee the Engine Room and support the engineers of the watch to do their jobs.

First Engineer/Senior Engineer-has the most experience out of all the engineers on board the ship and gets paid more. They usually are a day working engineer and oversees the two engineers on watch. They are there in the "pit" with his or her coveralls on if there is a problem.

Electrical Officer-you won't find an electrical officer on every ship but on larger vessels they oversee all the wiring and electrical instruments on board a vessel.

Second Engineer-usually has the night watch from midnight to noon as the more experienced engineer on watch. They operate and maintain the generators and propulsion plant when the ship is sailing.

Third Engineer-usually has the day watch from noon to midnight as they are less experienced and have the first engineer or chief engineer to back them up if need be. They operate and maintain the generators and engines when the ship is sailing.

Oiler-is an engine room assistant. They help with regular maintenance, do fluid level checks, and are there to assist the engineers on watch with anything they may need help with. They also do routine rounds to make sure there are no fires or floods in any engine compartments.

GALLEY STAFF:

Logistics Officer/Chief Steward-is ultimately in charge of the entire galley staff. They also do all the paperwork, purchase orders, and inventory, for the food and supplies onboard the ship.

Chief Cook/First Cook-oversees the galley and reports to the logistics officer who reports to the first mate or captain. He/she oversees meal planning, creating menus and cooking depending on how large the staff and vessel are.

Second Cook-is there to help the chief cook or first cook in preparing the meals and menus. They usually make things like salads and desserts if there is no pastry chef.

Steward-the steward/s are there to wash dishes, do laundry, and make bunks. They clean cabins for the mates, engineers and captain.

Keep in mind that every ship is different, and every ship has its own hierarchy onboard. This is just a basic list. Some ships like a navy ship or a cruise ship will have many more positions in between. Some smaller ships or boats may even combine positions like cook/deckhand. One major rule to remember on a ship is if someone is above you on the hierarchy scale, you always obey him or her when they give you an order.

Knots, Bends, and Hitches

Every good sailor knows how to tie knots. It's one of the most important things about being on a ship and going to sea. You never know when knots could save your life one day. Whether it is to tie a bowline in a hurry to throw to someone who has fallen overboard, or to tie a monkey's fist to toss a heaving line ashore in strong winds, knots are pretty much used for anything a sailor handles.

To understand knots, you should first understand rope. There are many kinds of rope made up of different materials, but the first thing to know is how rope is made. Rope is made up of different strands and woven into a larger tighter strand. Some of the materials used to make rope are stronger than others and are better used out in the elements. Natural fibers are more susceptible to breaking down by exposure to the sun if left out too long and some can even rot if wet and not properly taken care of. Natural rope needs to be hung up and stored in a dry area so that it's not exposed to the harsh elements.

Some types of natural rope are:

- **Manila**
- **Cotton**
- **Sisal**
- **Hemp**

Synthetic rope usually lasts longer and can be used for all purposes. There are many kinds of synthetic rope. They need to be treated with care as well because sun exposure can damage and bleach the synthetic fibers. As a rule of thumb, you should take care of all your rope as it may save your vessel or life one day. Rope can also get very expensive especially if you need buy a lot of it for a towline or an anchor line. It can usually be purchased by the foot at any marine store. Some types of synthetic rope are:

- **Spectra**
- **Nylon**
- **Kevlar**
- **Polyester**
- **Polypropylene**

One thing you need to be extremely careful of when using any type of rope but more so with synthetic, is that if you have it under max load it can spring back if it snaps. This could be very dangerous if it hits someone in the head it could even take your head off if you're not careful. A rope once snapped under a very heavy load and shot right past my head. I just stood there in shock as my fellow crew members came to see if I was OK. Boy was I lucky. With that much force and power behind it, a snapped line can do serious damage.

You also never want to stand in the "bight" of a line or rope. A bight is when you are between the two ends or loop of the rope. If you are dropping an anchor, for instance, and your foot is in the middle of the bight, you could very well go overboard with the anchor and end up in Davy Jones' Locker. Safety first!

The knot that every great sailor knows how to tie behind his or her back, in the dark, or in the water, is called the Bowline. There are a few different variations of the Bowline but is a knot that could end up saving your life one day. You can tie a Bowline on the end of a line and toss it to someone in the water. They can string it around them as you pull them in. You can also send a Bowline down a hole or cliff and if the person who is stuck loops it around themselves you can pull them up to safety. This knot really is a "safety knot" as some people call it.

There are so many different uses for the Bowline. You can also tie two pieces of line together to make a really long line, or it can even be used as part of a trucker's hitch to secure a load. A rope with a Bowline in it retains 65% of its original strength.

Below is a picture of a Bowline for your reference.

Photo credit-Terrance Lam Photography

A great hitch that comes in handy on a ship is a Round turn two half hitches. It's so easy that many people probably do it without even knowing it. It's a great way to hang up line or rope with the running end. You can even secure a line with it.

Photo credit-Terrance Lam Photography

A hitch that every great sailor should know is a Clove Hitch. Sailors use this hitch for securing an object to a bar or post. It consists of two half hitches put together and has two running ends.

Photo credit-Terrance Lam Photography

Another knot that is useful for cinching something tight is the Hangman's Noose. It can be used for something as big as a neck or bigger and can cinch right up to the size of the line. This would vary depending on the size of line you use. The knot gets its name from an obvious source as they used to use this knot for hanging people believed to be witches back in the day and for the death penalty as recent as 1996 in the U.S.

Photo credit-Terrance Lam Photography

Whippings

Whippings are used to finish the end of a line, so it doesn't come loose and to make it more aesthetically pleasing. You can use sailmaker's twine, which is usually pre-waxed. Below is the most popular whipping: The Common Whipping. There are many kinds of whippings more elaborate than the common whipping, but it does the trick nonetheless.

Photo credit-Terrance Lam Photography

Knot Board

Sailors quite often show off their decorative knot tying skills by creating beautiful works of art called Knot Boards. This is one way for a new sailor to learn all the names of the knots and hitches. The board is a great visual reference when a sailor tries out a knot for the first time. Below you will see a Knot Board from an old navy ship called the Lexington. This beautiful work of art would have taken hours to make with such tiny rope and fine details. This demonstrates precision in knot tying at its finest.

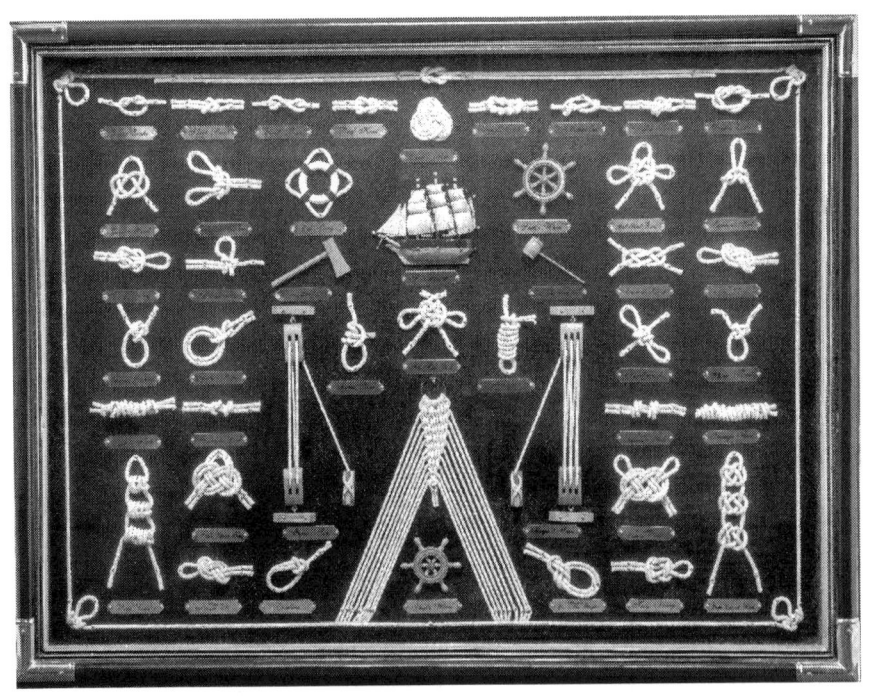

Photo credit-Terrance Lam Photography

As you can see, there are many different knots with uses for just about any purpose. A piece of line and a knife are all a sailor needs to be happy and can keep him or her busy for hours. This is what they call "busy work" or "make work" for those who are on the clock looking to kill some time.

All good sailors know how to sew with sailmaker's twine, a needle, and a leather palm. They can make anything from covers to sails and some sailors even make their own sea bag. The most common stitch is called the Blanket Stitch and can be used to sew canvas on a ship. I remember hand stitching covers for things like vents, so it protected it from the rain or from sea water getting inside. Blaine stitched a new canvas cover for the ship's log book to protect it from getting damaged. Other items you could make on a ship are pouches, also known as ditty bags, hammocks, sails, and so much more. The possibilities are endless!

Rules and Superstitions

Sailors are known for their superstitions when at sea or on a ship. There are many superstitions, but I will only list a few of the ones that I followed while onboard a ship.

Superstitions:

1. Never bring flowers on board a ship. They say that this is a bad omen because you can use the flowers for a funeral wreath or a burial at sea.

2. Do not bring any kind of large black duffle bag onboard as this could be used as a body bag.

3. Red sky in the morning, sailor's warning. Red sky at night, sailor's delight.

4. While on the bridge of a ship you should never whistle as it might "whistle up a storm".

5. To change a ship's name is extremely bad luck. I have heard many stories where a ship's name was changed, and the ship ended up sinking or floundering. I don't know if it was just a coincidence or not, but best be on the safe side and not change the ship's name as a rule of thumb.

Women at Sea

6. When you see rats fleeing a ship it is a pretty good indication to start running yourself as the ship is probably sinking or at the very least taking on water.

7. A sailor who dies at sea is said to go to Davey Jones' locker.

8. Women are bad luck on ships unless they are pregnant or naked. The naked thing is why a lot of ships have naked figurines carved on the bow of the ship. It is said if a baby is born at sea it is good luck. This is also where the term "son of a gun" comes from: a child of questionable parentage is either conceived or even born on the gun deck of a ship. (This superstition bothered me being a woman sailor. Obviously, times have changed and so things have changed, and women can work on and even command ships now).

9. To toss a coin to the sea before a ship departs the jetty is good luck, as it is paying a toll to the god Neptune for a safe voyage and safe return.

10. A ship is always referred to as a she for several reasons:

- **There is always a great deal of bustle around her.**
- **There is usually a gang of men about her.**
- **She has a waist and stays.**
- **It takes a lot of paint and maintenance to keep her looking good.**
- **It is not the initial expense that breaks you, it is her upkeep.**
- **She is all decked out.**
- **It takes an experienced man or sailor to handle her properly.**
- **Without a man at the helm, she cannot be controlled.**
- **Her topside is always showing, and she hides her bottom side.**
- **When coming into port, she always heads for the buoys.**

This is what they used to say in the old days. I think it's sexist to think some of these misogynistic comments anymore but are in many ways still true.

The hazing rituals at sea are usually done like the initiations of fraternities or sororities. It is also deemed payment to Neptune for becoming a sailor. This has been going on for hundreds of years and has been passed on for generations. Some rituals include men cross-dressing as women. Others involve drinking or crawling in something gross (worm at the bottom of a tequila bottle anyone?).

To give you a taste, for my initiation I had to snort Whisky up my nose. Yuck! I have never felt such a burning and stinging sensation all at once. It was not very pleasant. I guess they want to make sure you are tough enough to be a sailor as it is not an easy job. An initiation is a way to screen out the weak and the uninterested. The uninitiated are called Pollywogs; after you have been successfully initiated you become a Shellback.

Rules:

There are many rules aboard a ship, mostly to be respectful, and others that are strictly tradition. Some are ship specific and some are across the board. I have listed some rules here that were rules when I was aboard the ship to give you an idea as to what it was like. Again, it is not always the same on every ship.

1. Always obey your superior. There is a hierarchy onboard most vessels. Look for this in Hierarchy on a Ship (pg. 189).
2. Never call the captain by his/her first name. Always call them Captain Jones or refer to them as just plain "Captain".
3. Never be late when doing a watch change on the bridge. Especially when coming on to do a night watch

Women at Sea

you want to be there at least 15 minutes prior, to get your night vision before making the switch.

4. Never steal, fight, or sexually harass, anyone onboard the ship. Any one of these could be means for dismissal.

5. Never ring the ship's bell unless you are ringing in the New Year on New Year's Eve or are calling out the shots when heaving up the anchor line. This is usually only done by the boatswain or a leading seaman. You can also ring the bell continuously if you are in immediate danger.

6. When working on the deck, never walk or run across the deck when they have gear hanging over the side of the ship. This can be very dangerous, whether it be fishing gear, nets, or chain of any kind. If whatever is hanging over the side of the ship decides to let go suddenly and you are standing in the way, there is a very good chance you are going to be going right down to Davey Jones's locker with the rest of the gear.

7. Never wear rain gear or hats in the crew's mess. This goes for all government ships. A lot of times the punishment is to buy beer or pop for the crew. This is because the Queen's picture is usually hanging in the mess and it is proper etiquette and tradition to take off your hat in her "presence". Also, rain gear is just dirty and messy.

8. While up on the bridge as quartermaster on the ship's wheel, if you happen to hit a log it usually means you owe a beer or pop to the crew. This is not only entertaining but also means you were not doing your job as lookout up on the bridge, so it acts as a form of punishment too.

9. If you happen to be on the bridge in open water and spot a glass float (these are antique glass balls from Japanese fishing nets and they are worth a lot of

money) you are entitled to it. This happens once in a blue moon but when it does, consider yourself lucky.

10. Your crew members are like your brothers and sisters, never under any circumstances throw them under a bus or leave them high and dry. They will always be in your corner when the tough gets going so make sure you are always in theirs. This is sort of an unwritten rule that everyone should know and follow.

11. Never be late for breakfast, lunch, or dinner. It is disrespectful, and the cooks get mad if you are late because they can't eat until the rest of the crew eats. It also means they end up cleaning up later and in turn they leave the galley later.

12. Never be late when doing the "shakes" for the crew. A shake means to wake up the crew members with a knock on the door to make sure they show up for their watch. This is a tradition from way back when the only clock on board the ship was on the bridge and the night watch were the only ones who knew what time it was. Sometimes when you shake the Captain, they want to know what the weather is doing from the morning weather report. A shake is also helpful for your crew members that may need assistance waking up and making it on time for work.

13. Never ever under any circumstance drop or drag your country's flag on the ground when hoisting or taking down the flag. This is very disrespectful and very unpatriotic. This is a big NO-NO!

Astronomy 101

Did you know that some of the first sailors navigated at sea by the stars? Some of the better-known stars such as Polaris, otherwise known as the North Star, were an integral part of sailing and navigating, and are even still in use today. An instrument, such as the sextant that was invented in 1757, is still used as a traditional form of navigation, and the stars are used to measure the angle between two visible objects. This means you can find one's latitude and use the height of a landmark to determine or confirm a position on a nautical chart.

Sailors who wish to become watch keeping mates must take a full course on Astronavigation. There is a lot to learn in astronomy and a lot to know about Navigational Stars. There are 57 navigational stars that are some of the brightest stars found in the sky visible to the naked eye not including planets.

Bowdich's *American Practical Navigator* (Bowdich, N.1995), written by Nathaniel Bowdich, is one of the greatest nautical books ever published. There are several different volumes and it goes into depth about astronavigation and astronomy as every good sailor (especially those navigating the ship), should know how to locate themselves on a chart without the help of common navigational equipment in case they are ever lost at sea or have equipment malfunction.

There are so many different wonders of the world. I often looked up high above the clouds and gazed forever into the deep dark jet-black sky with millions of shiny sparkling balls of light staring back at me out on the open ocean. There is so much that we don't know about space and the stars, but the things we do know can help us better understand the world and life at sea.

In the old days, famous navigators relied heavily on the only things they could see at night and those were the twinkling bright shiny stars up above. Sailors could be weeks even months at sea sailing blindly across the open ocean. No radar, no GPS, no radio, no electronics, period. It's hard to imagine a world where none of those every day modern tools existed.

I often wonder what it was like being an early explorer at sea. The danger, the excitement of it all, the not knowing where you were going or where you would end up. To sail to a "new world" or a new land would truly be the experience of a lifetime and end up a pivotal moment in history. Some of the more well-known early explorers were known to carry compasses, a mariner's astrolabe (used to determine the ship's latitude from the sun or the stars, like a sextant), and a chip log (used to measure a ship's speed).

An old way of taking a depth sounding on a ship (before electronics) was to use a lead line made up of thin line with a small lead weight at the end. This weight had a small hole drilled from the bottom up and sailors would fill it with Tallow (solidified cow's fat), so that a sailor could tell what the make-up of the sea floor consisted of. The lead line would be marked every two-three fathom by different textiles such as leather or surge tied to the line. This was so that a sailor could tell just by eyeballing it how deep the line was to find the ship's depth.

We can learn a lot from our sailing ancestors by learning what tools they used and what they had to endure in their time. It never hurt anyone to have a back-up system in case your electronics fail while at sea. For me, learning old traditions is not only interesting but could also be useful one day. Gone are the days when everything was manual. Now

Women at Sea

you flick a switch and the machine does it all and calculates it for you.

Another useful tool when it comes to astronavigation is the nautical almanac. This book contains the coordinates of the earth's position in relation to the sun and other stars and planets for each hour of the year. You can use this guide to help you navigate the stars.

The Weather and Environment Conditions

The environment and weather conditions impact the life of a sailor greatly. Whether you are a fair-weather sailor, or a teeth-clenched, any-kind-of-weather kind of girl, you still need to do a sail plan in case something happens. Check the local weather beforehand for weather warnings, and assess the risks involved in going out to sea. A sail plan is a written plan stating where and when you will be leaving, your destination, and ETA (Estimated time of Arrival). Give your sail plan to someone you trust. If you don't check in with them when you are supposed to, ensure they call the local authorities/Coast Guard if you are overdue.

As part of our hourly rounds on the ship, we always had to finish on the bridge, take a weather reading, and record it into the ship's log book. This was to keep track of what the weather was doing to see if a weather pattern was forming. If there was a sudden drop in air pressure or if the wind was picking up, usually that meant a storm was coming.

The different kinds of storms you can come across on the ocean are:

Beaufort scale

Hurricane Force-Level 12 on the Beaufort scale
Violent Storm-Level 11 on the Beaufort scale
Storm Force-Level 10 on the Beaufort scale
Strong Gale-Level 9 on the Beaufort scale
Gale Force-Level 8 on the Beaufort scale
High Wind-Level 7 on the Beaufort scale
Strong Breeze-Level 6 on the Beaufort scale
Fresh Breeze-Level 5 on the Beaufort scale
Moderate Breeze-Level 4 on the Beaufort scale
Gentle Breeze-Level 3 on the Beaufort scale
Light Breeze-Level 2 on the Beaufort scale
Light Air-Level 1 on the Beaufort scale

You always need to be aware of the sea and swell. You should know what the sea state is, the difference between a 5ft. wave and a 30ft. wave and what that means for you. Unless you are an experienced sailor, I would recommend sticking to fair weather conditions while out on the water. Why risk it when you don't have to? Unless, of course, you are working and have no choice.

Clouds can also be an indicator of what the weather is doing. There are four different layers of clouds:

- **Cirrus** (curled)
- **Cumulous** (piled)
- **Nimbus** (bears rain)
- **Stratus** (spread out)

Each derives from a Latin term based on the shape of the cloud. Each type of cloud can originate from either a cold front or a warm front and will determine what kind of weather you get. If you make yourself familiar of what each type of cloud looks like, at least then it will help you be able to tell if a storm is coming while you are out on the water and hopefully be able to get to safety in time.

A good sailor also needs to know what to look for in detecting future problems and how to avoid them. For instance, if you see a deadhead sticking out of the water, in fact, you do not know how big it is. It could potentially be a whole tree for all you know. This could pose a potential risk if it were to shoot up out of the water beside your boat. Another good example is an iceberg. Up to 90% of the total size can be hidden underneath the water's surface and could potentially snag the side of your ship or boat. Take the Titanic, a tragic but educative example. The bottom side of the hull grazed against the underside of the iceberg causing the ship to sink.

A good lookout always knows what to look for. You can tell roughly how deep the water is just by common telltales. Deep water is usually a darker blue color whereas shallow water is a lighter green or turquoise. You may also tell if the water is shallow by the size of rocks in the vicinity, the vegetation around, and by what the waves are doing. To be a good lookout, you must use your sight and hearing the most, but it's not to say you shouldn't use all your other senses to guide you. You can also look and see if there are any other vessels in the area. If there are, figure out what they are doing, and it pays to look at what they are not doing.

There are rules and regulations on the water in place for the benefit of your safety as well as the benefit of other boaters. Local knowledge is the best knowledge, but if you are sailing in an area that is unknown to you and your crew, it's best to look at the charts and local weather thoroughly for that specific area before entering it.

Currents and eddies can be found anywhere and can be more prominent in certain areas. One such area is Cape Mudge, on northern Vancouver Island. Many lives have been lost at this location due to inclement weather or boating visitors coming and not knowing the local dangers. Please do your research and stay safe. Boating is fun but not when people get hurt.

Navigational aids are also there to help us stay consistently safe out on the water. If you have someone who is unfamiliar with the rules or that blatantly defies the rules on purpose, that's when accidents can and will occur. Of course, no one would want that to happen.

I once watched a boat go the wrong direction back into a harbor. Whoever was steering the boat didn't look at the buoys or the signage, and ended up grounding the keel on the sandbar and getting stuck. The Canadian Coast Guard Auxiliary, of which I was a member at the time, had to pull them off the sandbar and rescue them.

A good rule of thumb, and generally a good practice to follow, would be to strive to be prepared on the sea. One can never be too ready for whatever is to come. Be as safety conscious as you can, get the appropriate training and be in the know when it comes to the sea. If you are not prepared, you put yourself, your family, and others at risk.

Brianna Snider

Looking out from Whiffin Spit, Sooke, B.C.

-Photo Courtesy of B. Snider

Phonetic Alphabet

The Phonetic Alphabet is listed below. Each letter has a correlating nautical flag that also represents a different meaning. Most flags aren't commonly used anymore, except for a few: Alpha flag means "diver down, keep clear", the Bravo flag means "we're taking on or discharging dangerous cargo", and pilot boats use the Golf and Hotel flags which mean I require a pilot and I have a pilot onboard.

Phonetic Alphabet

A	Alpha	J	Juliet	S	Sierra
B	Bravo	K	Kilo	T	Tango
C	Charlie	L	Lima	U	Uniform
D	Delta	M	Mike	V	Victor
E	Echo	N	November	W	Whisky
F	Foxtrot	O	Oscar	X	X-ray
G	Golf	P	Papa	Y	Yankee
H	Hotel	Q	Quebec	Z	Zulu
I	India	R	Romeo		

I have learned this all by heart, as it is required to get your Radio Operator's License. If you are going to be using a VHF radio onboard any vessel it is required by law to get your license. The phonetic alphabet is used to avoid confusion when there is a language barrier as all mariners familiarize themselves with it and speak it clearly over the VHF. The global marine language is English. If you were going to choose a job or position working up in the bridge of a ship, such as a quartermaster, mate, or captain, you would want to get familiar with the Nautical Phonetic Alphabet.

⚓ Nautical Terminology

(A different language altogether)

The Nautical language is an extensive vocabulary of terms--almost a language unto itself. It is extremely important that you know what is being said when a superior is giving you direct orders, so you will need to study up if you will be working on board a ship. I have listed most of the important ones here so please take notes.

NAUTICAL TERMS and ACRONYMS

Abaft-Used when referencing abaft (behind) the beam

Abeam-A 90-degree angle to the orientation of the ship

Aboard-On board the vessel

Abreast-Alongside the vessel, or on the vessel's beam

Aft-Towards the back of the ship (also known as the stern)

Aloft-Refers to above the decks, including the mast, rigging, crow's nest, etc.

Amidships-An invisible line that runs right down the middle of the ship from the bow to the stern; a ship's wheel is said to be amidships when the ship's rudder is straight

Anchor Aweigh-When the anchor has been lifted off the sea bottom and the ship is now in control

Astern-The back or stern of the ship and behind the ship or moving backwards

Athwart ship- An invisible line 90-degrees from port to starboard

Beam-The largest width of a vessel from port to starboard

Bearing-Relative to either your compass (magnetic or gyro) or ship's bow

Belay-To cancel an order or a radio call; also, to secure or make fast a rope

Below-To be below the ship's decks

Bend-To tie a line or rope to a cleat, bitt, or onto another line

Berth-Where the ship docks; a bed or bunk

Bight-The middle of a loaded triangle made up of rope or chain also known as the danger zone; a cove or nook along the coast

Bioluminescence-The production and emission of light by a living organism. Some organisms living in the sea emit light, giving an appearance much like fireflies on land

Bitter End-The end of a line, rope or cable furthest away from the point you are working with

Bitts-Vertical posts where you can tie lines

Block-A piece of a pulley system where line runs through to help take a portion of the load

Boat hook-A long pole with a hooked end used for retrieving things from the water or pushing away from other vessels

Boatswain-The person in charge of the deck crew. He manages and directs all the deckhands, quartermasters, and leading seamen

Bow-The front end of the ship

Bridge-The command and navigation center of the ship

Bulkhead-A wall on a ship

Bulwarks-The top of the hull on the main deck of a ship

Bunk-A bed on a ship

Buoy-A piece of navigational equipment used by mariners for various purposes. There are many different shapes, sizes and colors of buoys each representing something different on the chart. Read the rules and regulations to better familiarize yourself

Cable-Equal to one-tenth of a nautical mile (185 meters)

Capsize (d)-When a vessel turns upside down in the water

Capstan-A revolving electrical device used to reel in heaving or mooring lines

Cast Off-To release lines from a dock

Chafing Gear-A protective sheath usually made from canvas or rope, used to prevent wear on mooring lines

Chart-A marine map

Cleat-A fixed piece of metal or wood used to secure lines

Course-The planned direction you are steering

Coxswain-The person in charge of a small boat

Crow's Nest-A lookout point on the top of the ship's mast

Dead Ahead-Directly in front of a vessel

Deadhead-A log or stump floating in the ocean, which can be very dangerous if struck with your vessel. Sometimes deadheads can be full trees or logs that have fallen off a log barge

Deck-The floor of a vessel

Deck Head-The ceiling of a vessel

Dinghy-A smaller "daughter" boat of a larger vessel. Often used in case of emergency and to travel to shore

Dog-To latch all doors, hatches, and portholes, to secure them

Draft-The distance from the waterline to the bottom of a ship's hull; the water used to float a vessel

Ease Off-To release tension on a line slowly

ETA-Estimated time of arrival

Fathom-A measurement of depth equal to 1.83 meters or six feet

Fairlead-Is a smooth hole where a line can run without chafing or snagging, mostly used for mooring lines

Fend Off-To prevent a ship from either touching another vessel or the wharf when coming in to port

Fix-A vessel's navigational position

Flying Bridge-The highest bridge on a vessel with more than one

Fo'c'sl-Is the upper most forward enclosure of the vessel

Foredeck-The deck most forward to the superstructure of the vessel

Foul-When lines or rope get "fouled" or tangled; it can also mean bad weather

Galley-A kitchen onboard a vessel

Guy-A supporting wire on a vessel

Hatch-A door/opening in the ship's deck to void space below also known as a hold where ship's stores are kept

Head-The vessel's toilet

Heading-The way the vessel is pointing at any given time

Headway-When the ship is moving forward with the engines running

Heave-To pull a rope or a line

Heave To-To slow down the ship to just being able to main steerage with hardly any headway

Helm-The ships wheel and electronics to steer the vessel

Hold-A storage area beneath the decks where ship's stores are kept

IMO-International Maritime Organization

Inshore-The direction towards the shore-line

Keel-What stabilizes a vessel under the hull. On sailboats, the keel is very long, on other vessels, the keel is more shallow

Ladder-A type of stairs you climb to get from one deck to another

Lash Down-To secure something by either tying it up with rope, chain

Lee-The side of the vessel furthest away from the wind (the sheltered side)

Leeward-The direction towards the lee side of the vessel

Leg-The middle part of the trip or cruise in between port A and port B

Line-Another term for a rope in use

Log-A book to keep a record of all ship's activities including trips/speed/persons on board/weather/etc.

Make Fast-To tie a line down and make it secure, usually to a cleat, or bitt, etc.

Marline-Twine that can be used for seizing, whippings, or to lash small objects down

Master-The commanding officer or captain of a vessel

MED-Marine Emergency Duties

Mess-Where the crew eat their meals, sleep, a bar, or a place to be entertained onboard the ship

Mile (Nautical)-Equal to 6,079 feet or 1,852 meters and an equivalent to one minute of latitude on a nautical chart

MOB-Man overboard

On the Beam-The direction of 90-degree off the bow or amidships of a ship

On the Bow-The direction of 45-degrees off the ship's bow or less.

On the Quarter-The direction of 45-degrees off the stern of the ship or less

OOS-Out of Service

Overboard-To be over a side of a vessel, often referred to as in the water

Painter Line-A line or rope attached to the bow of a small boat which is used for towing or tying the boat up

Part-To break referring to a line or rope breaking or snapping under strain

Payout-To let out rope or line, chain (anchor), or wire

Pilot-A shore-based navigator who works one specific harbor hired to navigate larger vessels into port that are unfamiliar with the area. They know every rock and hazard by heart in the area

Pitch-The motion of a ship when it goes back and forth opposed to side to side

Port-Left

Porthole-The equivalent of a window on a ship used for ventilation and to gaze out of, often above sea level

Quarter-Refers to the section of the ship that is forward of the stern and aft of the beam of the ship

Quarterdeck-The most aft part of the main deck on a ship also known as the stern area

Quartermaster-A seaman or deckhand who steers the ship's wheel as well as being a lookout on the bridge of a ship

Rail-The ledge on top of the bulwark

Reeve-To put a line through a block or a sheave

ROC-Restricted Operator Certificate (Radio certificate)

Roll-The angular motion in which a ship moves

RORO-Roll on roll off

Rules of the Road-The laws of navigation carried out by every good sailor to avoid collision

Running Lights-The lights shown when a vessel is underway, usually a red light on the port side, and a green light on the starboard side and one or two white light on the mast depending on the size of vessel

SAR-Search and Rescue

SCBA-Self Contained Breathing Apparatus (used for firefighting)

Sheave-A pulley on a vessel that helps lift heavy loads

SOLAS-Safety of Life at Sea (A system in place by the IMO to prevent deaths at sea)

Starboard-Right

Underway-When the ship is moving on the water

Unreeve-To withdraw rope from a block

Vessel-A floating object propelled by either sail or power also called a boat or a ship

VHF radio-Very High Frequency radio

Watch-A work shift usually four, eight, or twelve hours in length. Different ships have different watches depending on how they do things and how many crew are onboard

Weather-A difference in temperature and pressure, it is very important you know what the weather will be like before setting sail. You don't want to be caught in the middle of a storm

WHMIS-Workplace Hazardous Materials Information System

Winch-A machine used to pull line or wire

Windward-The direction the wind is coming from

Don't get discouraged if you don't pick up the lingo right away. As with any new vocabulary, it takes time. Practice does make perfect and soon you will be talking like a true sailor.

Now you are ready and have a basic knowledge of what it takes to become a sailor. I have covered some things to consider when deciding on a career at sea, and hope you find these last few chapters helpful in your journey. Good luck as you prepare for an adventure of a lifetime and be sure to enjoy the fresh sea air.

Meet the Contributors

Sandra Vandenham has since left the Royal Canadian Navy and is currently enjoying time off by travelling and going on adventures. She is always up for a challenge but doesn't think she will go back to sea

Carissa Tetreault now has two beautiful girls and goes back to sea on occasion. She is currently working for the Canadian Coast Guard in a shore position as a Marine Engineer

Laureen Bacon is currently enjoying retired life and travelling the world by other means such as cruise ships, jet planes, and motor homes. She no longer sails, but will always have a love of the ocean

Michelle Gendron is currently working for the Health Insurance B.C. as an Administration Clerk and has just started her own business as a photographer

Molly Peterson is not working on ships anymore. She went back to school to be a unit clerk in a hospital after trying her luck working in a shipping office ashore with no luck. When Molly is not in school, she loves playing with her new kitten

Channah Samuels is currently no longer going to sea and lives with her husband and two kids in Victoria, B.C.

Louise-Ann Granger is currently Superintendent of Marine Engineering working ashore with the Canadian Coast Guard, Western Region. She started her career at the Canadian Coast Guard College, graduated in 1993, spent nine years at sea on various CCG vessels on the West Coast and accumulated the sea time for the First Class Marine Engineering certification

Vanessa Downie is still actively going to sea working for the Canadian Navy and will continue to do so for the time being

Stacey Aikers still cooks on a fishing vessel and will continue to do so possibly until retirement now that her kids are grown and going to university

Alena Mondelli still works for the Canadian Navy. She has achieved the rank of Chief Petty Officer 1st Class and is looking forward to the many new adventures and challenges that will come

Stephanie Hamilton is currently doing a shore posting with the Navy but will return to sea after her two-year stint. She plans on staying at sea and working her way up through the ranks

Jackie Grant has currently just received her Master Mariners Certificate and lives with her husband and two kids on Vancouver Island

Jen Scott has taken a break from sailing and currently lives in North Saanich B.C. with her family

Paula White still works for the B.C Ferries out of Victoria, B.C. She has a husband and two beautiful little girls. She would like to continue to work for the ferries until she retires and is currently heavily involved with the Union of B.C Ferry workers

Heather Carlson had enough sea time to achieve her Master Mariners certificate. She no longer goes to sea and is home with her family in New Zealand

Karry Lowes is from Virginia, USA and is a Captain for hire. She loves to travel and to have adventures out on the water. She will continue going to sea until she can no longer physically do so

Jane Woo sailed the Great Lakes from 2008 – 2014. She no longer goes to sea anymore and is currently living in Saskatchewan with her husband

Sandy Hill is currently land-lubing it and teaching English in Mazatlan, Sinaloa, Mexico. She is trying to decide on leaving for a 1-2-year long cruise on the schooner Patricia Belle next spring

Heather Lee still races sail boats and is looking forward to her upcoming wedding this summer 2018

Nathalie Elliot is currently sailing as Chief Engineer on the CCGS Limonos on the east coast of Canada and will probably continue sailing until she retires

Captain Laura Nelson Is currently a professor at Resiolve Maritime academy teaching Dynamic Positioning. She currently holds her Chief Mate unlimited, Oceans license and DP unlimited. She is in line to receiving her Master Unlimited Oceans this February 2018. She currently resides in Florida, USA

Elize Duggleby worked as an Engineer for the Canadian Coast Guard for four years and plans to continue working in the marine industry. She currently lives in Victoria, B.C.

Girija Edwards is retired from B.C. Ferries, loves to travel, and loves to spend time with her kids and grandkids on the Sunshine Coast. She currently lives in Gibson, B.C.

Jack LeMaistre started working as a first mate doing a Sail Training Program around the Gulf Islands after returning to Canada from Nicaragua. She enrolled in school to obtain her Master Limited; 60ton ticket. She spent a season training as a Captain, and is due to start training with a new company in 2018. She is happily living with an incredible man and his lovely twin boys who love the sea as much as she does

Cynthia Thomas is currently working at a private company ashore. She enjoyed her time at sea when she was younger and wishes she could have made going to sea her full time career, but knows things happen for a reason. She is grateful to be with her husband and three beautiful girls today. She currently lives in Victoria, B.C.

Photo credit-Blaine Snider

About the Author

Brianna Snider is currently working for the Canadian Coast Guard in an administrative position. She has a loving husband and two kids who are her pride and joy. Her hobbies are camping, gardening, hiking, writing, laughing and spending time with her kids.

Even though she doesn't go to sea anymore, she still loves the smell of the salty sea air and she will always be a sailor at heart. Brianna lives with her husband and two kids in Victoria, B.C.

Acknowledgments

First, I would like to thank my parents Jacques and Laureen for always being there, believing in me and supporting me. I wouldn't be anywhere without their love and encouragement. I would also like to thank my little sister Melissa for always being there for me, and always being someone, I can talk to. I wouldn't be anywhere without the love and support of my husband Blaine and our two kids, Sienna and Kohan. They believed in me no matter what and put up with me and my writing into the wee hours of the morning. Writing your first book is a grueling task, especially with two small children. A big thanks to all my wonderful friends and family for all your continued support.

Special Thanks

Special thanks, to Carissa Tetrault for your continued support and advice through this journey and being the first woman, I interviewed.

Special thanks to Kevin Mah, Paula White, Vanessa Downie, Barbara Hodgson, and Katherine Slingsby for sending people my way to interview.

Big thank you to Val and Derek Morrison, Monique Bacon, Daniel and Linda Bacon, for housing me during my studies and during my visit to Quebec that helped get me into Sailor School so that I could become a sailor!

To Bill & Anne Kelly thank you for all your continued support and answering any questions I had throughout the challenging process of writing my first book.

Big thank you to Kate and John Guthrie for letting me borrow your camera for some of the photos!

Special thanks to Joanne McNish and Roger Girouard from the Canadian Coast Guard for your advice and encouraging words.

A very special thank you to Jackie Rioux and Sandra Ruttan for helping to edit and give me continued advice on my book.

To all the wonderful women who let me interview you or wrote stories for me to publish in this book, I truly couldn't have done this without you. It was truly a pleasure to meet you all and hear all your amazing sailing stories. Thank you all for helping my dream book come true.

References

1. Ayres, A. (1996). *Wit and Wisdom of Eleanor Roosevelt*: Penguin Group
2. Bloom, Harold. (1987). *William Shakespeare's measure for measure.* New York: Chelsea House.
3. Bowdich, N. (1995). *Bowdich American Practical Navigator an epitome of navigation,* Bethesda, Maryland, National Imagery and Mapping agency.
4. Rombauer, Irma S.; Marion Rombauer Becker *(1967 printing). Joy of Cooking (hardbound) (1964 ed.).* Indianapolis, Indiana: Bobbs-Merrill (Toronto: McClelland and Stewart Limited Edition)
5. Roosevelt, D.F. (1882-1945)
6. Sinetar, M. (1989). *Do What You Love, The Money Will Follow: Discovering Your Right Livelihood.* Dell; Reissue edition
7. Tolkien, J.R.R. (1954-1955). Lord of the Rings: *The Fellowship of the Ring; The Two Towers; The Return of the King.* United Kingdom: Allen & Unwin

Share with Us

If you are a woman sailor and would like to share your story with us, please contact womenatsea@gmail.com or visit our website at www.womenatsea.ca with any questions and or submissions. We would love to hear from you!

Women at Sea

Brianna Snider

Made in the USA
Columbia, SC
27 April 2018